AMERICAN TRADEMARKS:
A COMPENDIUM

EDITED BY

ERIC BAKER AND TYLER BLIK

CHRONICLE BOOKS
SAN FRANCISCO

Library of Congress Cataloging-in-Publication Data available.

ISBN 978-0-8118-7220-1

Manufactured in China.

p.2, 1935, The American Tobacco Co.; p.5, 1925, Edgar-Morgan Co.; p.8, 1928, Silent Automatic Corp.; p.10, 1954, Cleaver-Brooks Co.; p.12, 1937, Socony-Vacuum Oil Co. Inc.; p.52, 1955, Viking Sports Products, Inc.; p.68, 1946, Winters Brothers Co., p.110, 1975, Golden Dawn Foods, Inc.; p. 142, 1953, Robotron Corp.; p.158, 1952, System Trachtenberg; p.178, 1970, Loveland Skiing Corp.; p.194, 1938, Adam Hat Stores, Inc.; p.234, 1976, American Revolution Bicentennial Administration.

10 9 8 7 6 5 4 3 2 1

Chronicle Books LLC
680 Second Street
San Francisco, CA 94107
www.chroniclebooks.com

AMERICAN TRADEMARKS:
A COMPENDIUM

ACKNOWLEDGMENTS

We would like to thank all the people who have helped bring this book to life. Very special thanks go to Amy Wu, the very best assistant one could ever dream of; Brian Pelayo, who was a huge help in minding all the details and minutia; Steve Heller for his continued interest and passion; and to all our designer friends and colleagues whose contributions have provided a contemporary link and perspective to this historical collection of American trademarks.

At Chronicle Books: Michelle Dunn Marsh, Michael Carabetta, Becca Cohen, Eloise Leigh, and Bridget Watson Payne; thank you all so much for the support, encouragement and care.

We would also like to salute the many anonymous designers and artists whose work in this book has provided so much admiration, inspiration, and joy.

Lastly, much love to our families: Bonnie, Lena, and Sasha; and Sonya, Alek, and Naomi, as they make everything meaningful.

ERIC BAKER AND TYLER BLIK

My Friends, the Trademarks

I never realized I had so many friends until now. I'm not talking about sentient human buddies but rather the logos and trademarks in this book. "Get a life," you say? Believe me, I know where you're coming from. But seriously, the best marks are meant to be more than a graphic representation of a business, institution, or organization; they are supposed to be indelibly etched into our individual and collective consciousness (and subconsciousness too). They are supposed to evoke those Proustian moments and Pavlovian responses that force us to feel and act. They are the trigger for a wide array of responses that would not be activated if not for their familiarity and ubiquity. They are our friends, or at least they claim to be.

Of course, some—perhaps many—logos and trademarks fail at this desired result. For any number of reasons a mark can misfire, even hurt us and become our enemy. The worst examples are patently obvious—the Swastika, for instance, or Enron (although it didn't start out that way). A mark is only as good a friend as the corporation or concept that it represents enables it to be. Yet once positively established in the mass mind, it is potentially as near and dear to us as any other personal treasure.

This waxing on about logo and trademark intimacy may seem a little—or a lot—hyperbolic and unrealistic. However, the fact is we live in a marked culture. Brands are determinants in how our lives are lived, what we strive for, how we measure success and happiness. Our marks, backed by expensive promotion and incessant buzz, are our guideposts. "When's he going to invoke religion?" you ask. Well, it is hard not to look at commercial, institutional, and ideological marks as part of a continuum that leads back to the earliest religious signs and symbols. And if you don't want to go back that far, look at the merchants' crests of old. Such icons were seals of authority, power, and thus credibility. Today hundreds of their descendants are marks of status sewn on our products and tattooed on our bodies.

Getting back to friendship. This book is like a big reunion. As an updated compendium of the authors' previous volumes, it is a reuniting of a vast store of material that for over two decades many designer friends have used as a resource. When Eric Baker and Tyler Blik issued their first volume, designers seemed hungry for inspiring visual stimuli. The design world was pinging and ponging between Modernists on one side and Postmodernists on the other. Somewhere in between were eclectics who cherry-picked inspiration from both sources, and others too. Vintage trademarks provided raw material from which some designers created hybrids and others simply copied.

Baker and Blik's first and second volumes fueled the "retro" aesthetic and were part of a string of vintage mark, type, and design books (to which I contributed a few, too). In this way it was a rest home for old friends. It was as comforting to peruse the collection of marks as it is to, sometimes, experience an old photo album. These graphic relics came from a period before CI (corporate identity) was governed by Modernist marketing principles and branding became the buzzword of the moment. Most of these marks were created by craftsmen; some in art service studios; others were freelance draftsmen; and still more were trained, illustrious commercial artists whose names are long forgotten. Although these were deliberately created for businesses large and small, somehow because they are "anonymous" and do not conform to the established or sophisticated Modernist modes, they have been labeled "vernacular," as in indigenous to the culture in which they were produced.

Yet they are not so innocent or indigenous. Even some of the goofier examples were "worked." We will probably never know whether there were one or one hundred sketches and iterations. But as much as we'd like to label them as folk art—which makes them so much friendlier, and copyright free—they were made for a specific purpose to identify and brand a particular entity. Still, time has had its way with them. Styles have changed and what was a "smart" mark fifty or more years ago is, well, a "dumb" mark today. It is inconceivable that a contemporary corporation can have a successful international identity by employing a trade character or mascot. Helvetica was created to avoid the quirky, eccentric personalities that early industrialists seemed to be fond of. But that quirkiness is why we embrace many of the marks in this book as friends.

We are quite comfortable working with them too. They are not upstarts. They don't have attitude. They fit nicely into certain quaint design solutions, or can be sampled to give a glimmer of idiosyncrasy to others. And even if we choose not to repurpose them in contemporary designs, we get enjoyment from the mere fact of their existence. Friends are like that. They don't have to say or do anything, but if you feel close enough, all they have to do is be there.

When these compendia were published for the first time, the design world was a different place. The computer was in its infancy. It was unclear how it would be used. Graphic design was also ascending as a creative service field. Despite the two dominant *isms*, anything went, and these trademarks were part of "the big closet" that Tom Wolfe called the reference bin from which designers plumbed their ideas. Today, the demands on designers have shifted. "Anything goes" has kind of gone. Retro is either a guilty pleasure or a besmirched excuse for lack of original thinking. The marks here may or may not inspire an old or new direction, but as friends they are still worth their weight in gold.

STEVEN HELLER

A Dialogue Between Generations

How does this visual compendium of historical trademarks create such an interesting thread to the continually evolving aesthetic and the numerous cultural references America has possessed? As professional communicators and designers, we of course relish in the nuances of what each trademark might express, perhaps even borrowing a form, a style, or an idea for our own use. But there is something much more significant about what these marks collectively represent to all of us. They are iconic ghosts, spirits of what we've been, as well as road maps to how we will communicate with each other in the future. To quote the late, great educator, author, and graphic design historian, Philip Meggs, "Trademarks become miniature worlds that store memories, passions, and reputations in the minds of employees, customers, and stockholders." And we might also add, "society as a whole."

In 1983, when we first began work on the original edition of *Trademarks of the '20s and '30s*, the world of design was a different place. Most of the things we take for granted did not exist. It was a world where computers were in their infancy. There was no design software and the first Macintosh had not yet appeared in the marketplace. There was no e-mail, the Internet was used solely by the government (Arpnet), fax machines were rare and cost thousands of dollars, and, by today's standards, cell phones were clumsy devices that cost $8 a minute to use.

As designers, there were a few coveted periodicals or annuals to peruse, but there was not the plethora of design-related books we see today. If you needed to do research you went to the local public or private library to see what you might uncover. Ideas typically evolved from numerous sketches and refinement by way of "tissues." Typesetters, color houses, and many other craftspeople all provided a hand of expertise in the long and laborious process of getting something to print on press. It wasn't any different with our initial research, design, and publication of these trademarks. As this newly edited and formatted edition came together, many wonderful memories from those days began to surface. As young designers in our twenties and with one slightly valid credit card between us, we convinced the San Diego Public Library to let us take out the only known (reference) volumes on the west coast of the U.S. Patent Office's publication—the Official Gazette. The library required us to check out no more than one year's material at a time, yet these massive books, each representing a month of the patent office's work, became a tedious effort in hauling them from library to car, to late-at-night studio darkroom and back again. to record our discoveries.

Although the process was long and many times delayed because of the scuttle between library research, our full-time design jobs, and overall inexperience, patterns of these trademarks started to unfold. We became just as excited in discovering the naïve and often-humorous cultural vernacular as we were with the well-designed and aesthetic ones. We began to not only look at this as a design exercise, but as an anthropological one—discovering the many historical milestones of our human behavior and the ever-expanding and evolving technologies of American commerce and culture.

As we continued to observe and critique these visual treasures, various themes began to emerge. Trademarks representing America's early agricultural roots, iconic heroes, transportation needs, unique colloquial phrasing, new technologies, the atomic age, expansion of entertainment, and the unfolding of corporate America all provided glimpses of the amplification of human ingenuity and the speed at which we, as a nation, were traveling. Each decade of trademarks revealed something uniquely new, a continuous impression of our creative and social psyche.

We never expected the original books to enjoy the success they did, nor did we expect them to have such an influence on contemporary graphic design. We were just happy to have them published and see them in bookstores. Graphic designers were just beginning to evolve their expressions beyond the cold, geometric, and "corporate" style that seemed to prevail at that time. We were somewhat unprepared, but *Trademarks of the '20s and '30s* seemed to be just the right tonic young designers were searching for at that time. Soon after its release, knockoffs began showing up everywhere. Certain marks were appropriated and re-purposed in the first *Batman* movie, on TV shows, as fashion brands, in advertising, and of course, by other designers who even claimed awards through their slight modifications. Imitation can be the sincerest form of flattery to these old stalwart trademarks, but was it appropriate?

Today, almost 25 years later, everything has changed. Or has it? Certainly our access to visual materials is much greater. We have the ability to produce work faster and with greater variation and there are more designers than ever. But an idea is still paramount to the creative process and its resonance with its audience. Revealing that history becomes more important than ever. Everything old is new again. To younger designers these marks are "vintage" or "retro," but with a closer look we see the reflection and spirit of the time in which they were created. We can see how culture has evolved and how designers were truly agents of change. It is our hope in reintroducing these "miniature worlds" that new generations of designers will gain a better understanding of their legacy and the evolution of their profession.

ERIC BAKER AND TYLER BLIK

ANIMALS

1925, M. Halff & Brothers,
San Antonio, TX.
Bleached Woven Cotton Cloth.

1932, Belmet Products, Inc.,
Brooklyn, NY.
Portable Shoulder Shower.

1938, U.S. Rubber Products, Inc.,
New York, NY.
Rubber Bathing Caps, Rubber
Girdles, and Rubber Bathing Suits.

1920, Aberdeen Packing Co.,
Aberdeen, WA.
Canned Salmon.

**1932, The Great Atlantic
& Pacific Tea Co.,**
New York, NY.
Canned Salmon.

1925, B. H. Hakstad & Co.,
Chicago, IL.
Cod Liver Oil.

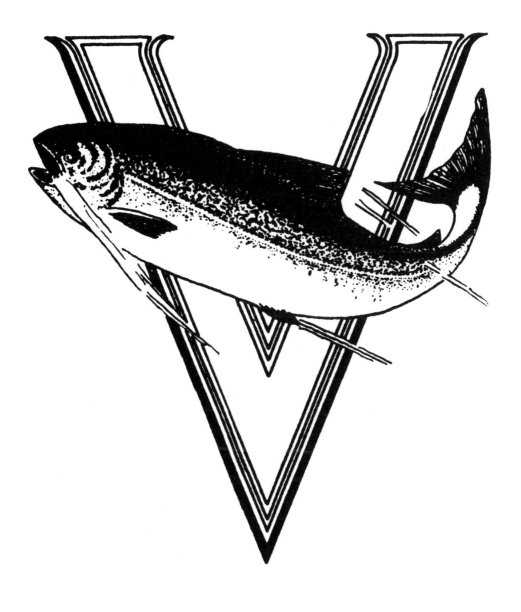

1935, Fidalgo Island Packing Co., Seattle, WA. Canned Salmon.

1925, Chemisch-Pharmazeitische Fabrik,
Berlin, Germany.
Perfumery and Cosmetics.

1938, Davenport Hosiery Mills, Inc.,
Chattanooga, TN.
Hosiery.

1938, Julius Schmid, Inc.,
Aberdeen, WA.
Canned Salmon.

1938, Rider Safety Razor Co.,
New York, NY.
Razor Blades and Pocket Knives.

1925, Nitrate Agencies Co.,
New York, NY.
Fertilizer.

1939, Arctic Roofings, Inc.,
Edge Moor, AK.
Composition Shingles
and Roll Roofing.

1936, Harrington & Waring,
New York, NY.
Hosiery.

1935, West's Products Co.,
Milwaukee, WI.
Bird Seed.

1928, Lineol Aktiengesellschaft,
Brandenburg-on-the-Havel, Germany.
Toy Soldiers, Toy Animals,
Toy Menageries.

1922, Washburn-Crosby Co.,
Minneapolis, MN.
Semolina and Durum Wheat Flour.

1925, Sun Soap Products, Inc.,
Staten Island, NY.
Soap Powders.

1925, Jersee Co.,
Minneapolis, MI.
Egg Mash for Poultry.

1935, Birdseye Electric Co.,
Gloucester, MA.
Electric Incandescent Lamps
and Radio Vacuum Tubes.

1929, The Federal Washboard Co.,
Tiffin, OH.
Washboards.

1936, Pennsylvania Rubber Co, Inc.,
Jeannette, PA.
Shuttlecocks.

1930, Harry C. Eisenhut,
Richmond Hill, NY.
Bird Food.

1936, Braided Fabric Co.,
Providence, RI.
Knitting Bags, Bathing Bags, Tourist
Bottle Kits, Shopping Bags.

**1927, American Seed
and Food Products,**
Chicago, IL.
Bird and Aquarium Supplies.

1936, Lydia V. Billing, Piedmont, CA. Hair Grower.

FAIRCHILD

1929, Fairchild Aviation Corp., New York, NY. Internal-Combustion Engines.

1928, Milwaukee Grains & Feed Co., Milwaukee, WI. Horse and Dairy Feeds.

1938, Pepperell Manufacturing Co.,
Boston, MA.
Fabrics Made of Cotton, Silk,
Rayon, and Artificial Silk.

1925, Belle City Manufacturing Co.,
Racine, WI.
Thrashing Machinery, Tractors,
Silo Fillers, and Feed Cutters.

1931, Mayflower Mills,
Fort Wayne, IN.
Wheat, Phosphated,
and Self-Rising Flours.

1925, Kenworthy Grain & Milling Co.,
Tacoma, WA.
Stock and Poultry Feed.

1934, Herman Sanders,
St. Louis, MO.
Lactic Preparation for Use
as a General Bodybuilding Tonic.

1927, Maurice L. Rothschild, Inc.,
Chicago, IL.
Shoes Made of Leather.

1937, Suffolk Brewing Co.,
Boston, MA.
Cereal Malt Beverage.

1928, Francis H. Legget & Co.,
New York, NY.
Breakfast Cocoa, Sweet Relish,
Catsup, Olives, and Mixed Pickles.

1934, W. R. Arthur & Co. Inc.,
Chicago, IL.
Lubricant Oils.

1925, Empire Milling Co., Minneapolis, MN. Hog Feed.

1924, Allwood Lime Co., Manitowoc, WI. Hydrated Lime.

1935, National Coast Products Corp., Swedesboro, NJ. Canned Dog and Cat Food.

Charles Anderson
CHARLES S. ANDERSON DESIGN COMPANY

I have some old notions about logos drilled into my head by my MCAD (Minneapolis College of Art and Design) professor and first employer, Peter Seitz. Peter's views were influenced by his own design education, which began at the New Bauhaus in Ulm, Germany, under Max Bill and Otl Aicher, and then at Yale where he studied under Paul Rand, Herbert Matter, and Bradbury Thompson. Peter worked as a graphic designer for architect I. M. Pei and later held the position of design curator at the Walker Art Center in Minneapolis. Peter Seitz taught us that a logo should be simple, distinct, memorable, reducible, reproducible, appropriate, and timeless. He also believed that a logo must work in black and white.

My late 1970s Swiss Modern Design education clashed dramatically with my love of comic books and other lowbrow illustration influences that didn't fit into MCAD's modernist design ideology. To this day, I still struggle to find balance by combining simple, bold, figurative logos with formal grid structures, classic typography, and modern compositions. An illustration can be used as a logo, but perhaps not very effectively due to the fact that most illustrations are not simple, iconic, reducible, or timeless. On the other hand, I am not necessarily an advocate of the geometric, abstract logo that is supposed to express everything about a company but really says nothing. These abstract dingbats may be simple, iconic, timeless, reducible, and reproducible, but they are often not distinct or memorable, and can be viewed as cold, lifeless, and generic. What I've discovered over the past three decades is that a strong logo that fulfills all seven Seitz requirements is extremely difficult to create and over time can grow to become a corporation's most valuable asset.

1997, Betty Crocker.

2007, French Environmentalism.

2006, French Paper Company.

2008, Halifax Health.

1998, Nike Baseball.

2000, Tiger Woods Nike.

1991, Turner Classic Movies.

2009, Mr. French.

1999, Warner Bros.

1958, The M. Norton Co.,
Troy, NY.
Pressure-Sensitive Adhesive Tapes.

1946, Bear Manufacturing Co. Inc.,
Chicago, IL.
Automobile Wheels, Tools,
and Racks.

1950, Behr-Manning Corp.,
Troy, NY.
Adhesives.

1957, The Howard Zink Corp.,
Freemont, OH.
Life Preserver Cushions and Jackets.

1944, The Fishery Council,
New York, NY.
Fresh, Canned, Frozen, Shredded,
Salted, Dried, and Pickled Fish.

1948, C. S. Williamson & Co.,
Orangeburg, SC.
Fish Stringer.

1950, Gonda Engineering Co., Inc.,
Salem, OH.
Tricycles.

1955, J. William Horsey Corp.,
Plant City, FL.
Frozen Concentrated Orange Juice.

1958, Outboard Marine Corp.,
Waukegan, IL.
Outboard Motors and Repair Parts.

1951, Town & Farm Co., Inc.,
Papillion, NE.
Radio Program Broadcasting.

1940, Welch Fruit Products Co.,
Chicago, IL.
Non-Alcoholic, Non-Cereal,
Maltless Beverages.

1947, Keyston Brothers,
San Francisco, CA.
Automotive Seat Covers,
Springs, and Hinges.

1956, Matco Transportation, Inc., Brooklyn, NY. Truck Transportation Services.

1954, Arbie Mineral Feed Co., Inc.,
Marshalltown, IA.
Mineralized Hog Feed.

1954, Piggly Wiggly Corp.,
Jacksonville, FL.
Coffee, Tea, Eggs, Beans, Spices,
and Other Packaged Food.

1954, The Sanitary Market,
Rogers City, MI.
Smoked Pork Loins.

**1958, Barbeque Queen
Food Systems,**
Los Angeles, CA.
Barbeque Sauce and Salad Dressing.

1957, Urban N. Patman, Inc.,
Los Angeles, CA.
Packages Containing Servings of
Fresh Beef, Lamb, and Pork.

1958, The Burk Co.,
Philadelphia, PA.
Canned and Smoked Meats, Lard.

1935, National Coast Products Corp., Swedesboro, NJ. Canned Dog and Cat Food.

1940, King Novelty Co., Chicago, IL. Paints and Painters' Materials.

1947, Armour & Co.,
Chicago, IL.
Fertilizer.

**1956, Screen Directors' Guild
of America,**
Hollywood, CA.
Entertainment Services.

**1950, New York Herald
Tribune, Inc.,**
New York, NY.
Daily Newspaper.

1955, Manuel Ortiz, Jr.,
Sarasota, FL.
Radios, Phonographs, and
Recording Sound Amplifiers.

1953, The Gummed Products Co.,
Toledo, OH.
Heat Seal Papers.

**1956, Container Corporation
of America,**
Chicago, IL.
Paperboard Shipping Containers.

1954, Richfield Oil Corp.,
New York, NY.
Gasoline, Oil, and Greases.

1948, Bell & Zoller Co.,
Chicago, IL.
Coal.

1949, Eagle Lock Co.,
Terryville, KS.
Door Closers.

1950, The Rath Packing Co.,
Waterloo, IA.
Dressed Young Turkeys,
Chickens, and Fowl.

1956, Nichols Poultry Farm, Inc.,
Kingston, NH.
Hatching Eggs and Day-Old Chicks.

1948, North Carolina Finishing Co.,
Salisbury, NC.
Treating Textiles for
Water Resistance.

1954, Glovercraft, Inc.,
Johnstown, NY.
Men's Leather Jackets.

1955, Spartan Mills,
Spartanburg, SC.
Kitchen Towels, Tablecloths,
Napkins, and Place Mats.

1949, American Bank Note Co.,
New York, NY.
Intaglio, Lithography, Embossing,
and Printing Services.

1947, Norbert Jay,
New York, NY.
Packaging and Product Designing.

1951, Mathieson Chemical Corp.,
Baltimore, MD.
Insecticides.

1957, Dri Dux Co.,
Lodi, NJ.
Water- and Mildew-Repellent
Coatings.

1955, Sassy Dog and Cat Food Co., Long Beach, CA. Cat and Dog Food.

1947, Cat's Paw Rubber Co., Inc. Chelsea, MA. Men's, Women's, and Children's Rubber-Sole Shoes.

1958, Walt Disney Music Co., Burbank, CA. Phonograph Records.

Aaron Draplin
DRAPLIN DESIGN COMPANY

My favorite logos are found on old things that usually get thrown away.

When it comes to trademark design, I'll forever be inspired by heavies like Saul Bass, Lance Wyman, Lester Beall, and Paul Rand. Their geometry, restraint, and wit is that of legend, and I fight hard to exhibit their time-tested sensibilities in my own work.

But those guys get enough press, so I'm gonna rant about the "unsung heroes of logo design"—or "the folks who make the stuff that is often overlooked, and far from celebrated in glossy design books: the designers of no-bullshit logos found on old stuff in garages and basements." That might sound a little vague, but that's the best way I can put it.

I'll be at some estate sale or garage sale, battling middle-aged eBay parasites, scared arachnids, and bored ghosts, and I'm elbow-deep in some old workshop cabinet and I'll be stopped in my tracks by an old package of forgotten hardware.

And on that package will be a logo representing whatever company made the nail, fuse, or ball bearing that it holds. Completely straightforward and devoid of any pretension, their sole objective was to set themselves apart from the other packages on the shelf at the hardware store. And what a job they did. Garages from 1950 must have been beautiful, considering the garbage you are forced to buy at Home Depot nowadays.

So yeah, there's a lot to be learned from the celebrated masters of logo design. But equally, there's a wealth of greatness to be discovered on things that are hidden in old cupboards and tackle boxes. If you know how to look, you'll find 'em. Be warned: You gotta get dirty.

While my scavenging competitors are tussling over cast iron skillets and glassware, I'm perfectly content rescuing this stuff from a certain death in a landfill or incinerator. And to whoever designed the "International Rectifier Semiconductors" logo on that old radio component package I rescued from that shed in Spokane last week, well, I applaud you.

2007, DDC Open Road Div.

2007, Suburban Blend.

2008, Cobra Dogs.

2004, Union Binding Co.

2007, Exit Real World.

2005, Re:volve.

2005, Longbreed Gary.

2008, Redwing Farms.

2004, Nike Air Max.

1968, Swanee Paper Corp.,
New York, NY.
Bathroom Tissues, Facial Tissues,
Paper Napkins, and Paper Towels.

1961, Youngs Rubber Corp.,
New York, NY.
Condoms.

1974, Subsea Equipment, LTD.,
Hamilton, Bermuda.
Equipment for Subsea Oil
and Gas Installations.

1979, Stanley H. Kaplan,
New York, NY.
Educational Services.

1974, Motel Corporation of America,
Georgetown, Grand Cayman Island.
Motel, Hotel, Inns, and Campsites.

1955, HMH Publishing Co., Inc.,
Chicago, IL.
Monthly Magazine.

1978, Ralston Purina Co.,
St. Louis, MO.
Animal Feed.

1974, Relim Publishing Co., Inc.,
Chicago, IL.
Magazines.

1978, Ralston Purina Co.,
St. Louis, MO.
Dog Food.

1971, Burton G. Feldman, Chicago, IL. Copying Services.

1975, Panangling, LTD.,
Chicago, IL.
Travel Agency Services.

**1975, Volkswagenwerk
Aktiengesellschaft,**
Wolfsburg, Germany.
Automobiles.

1956, Richter Co., Inc.,
New York, NY.
Candles.

1965, California Western Railroad,
Fort Bragg, CA.
Steam-Powered Rail Transportation
of Persons and Property.

plaf

1966, Geigy Chemical Corp.,
Ardaley, NY.
Sponges.

1956, Nixalite America,
Davenport, IA.
Bird and Rodent Barrier Structure.

1973, William C. Hunt,
Issaquah, WA.
Multipurpose Cooking Assembly.

1977, Farmstead Industries,
Waterloo, IA.
Prefabricated Livestock Pens.

1969, Trimfoot Co.,
St. Louis, MO.
Infant's Shoes.

1962, Star-Kist Foods, Inc.,
Terminal Island, CA.
Canned Fish.

1969, Consolidated Foods Corp.,
Chicago, IL.
Frozen Fish and Seafood.

Farmer Ell-Dee

1977, McMullen Grove Co.,
Riverview, FL.
Tropical Fish and Aquatic Plants.

1960, Hayes Spray Gun Co., Pasadena, CA. Service Kit Comprising Replacement and Repair Parts for Garden Spray Guns.

1960, Birmingham Tin Shop, Birmingham, AL. Small Gasoline Powered Autos.

1967, Eddie Bauer, Seattle, WA. Waterfowl Decoys.

PETIT PIGEON

1963, Petit Pigeon, La Jolla, CA. Mail Order Sales of Clothing and Accessories.

1962, Walter Lantz Productions,
Hollywood, CA.
Woody Woodpecker
Chewing Gum.

1976, Host International, Inc.,
Santa Monica, CA.
Raw Chicken and Chicken Parts.

1965, The Coca-Cola Co.,
Atlanta, GA.
Canned Fruit Juices and
Fruit Juice Drinks.

**1966, Aberdeen
Manufacturing Corp.,**
New York, NY.
Umbrellas and Parts Thereof.

1969, Cassandra Record Co.
Huntington Beach, CA.
Musical Recordings and Records.

1967, Lynden Farms, Inc.,
Seattle, WA.
Poultry Products.

1967, Chick-Fil-A, Inc.,
Hapeville, GA.
Frozen Chicken Parts.

1937, Suffolk Brewing Co.,
Boston, MA.
Cereal Malt Beverage.

1967, Austin E. Meyers,
Denver, CO.
Restaurant Services.

1969, Cardinal Vending Co.,
Cleveland, OH.
Vending Machines.

1971, Devonshire Melba Corp.,
Carlstadt, NJ.
Melba Toast.

1971, Ptarmigan Inn, Inc.,
Steamboat Springs, CO.
Motel Services.

1975, Continental Can Co.,
New York, NY.
Paperboard and
Corrugated Paper Boxes.

1973, Suffolk Brewing Co.,
Boston, MA.
Cereal Malt Beverage.

**1974, The Mennonite Publishing
House, Inc.,**
Scottdale, PA.
Non-Technical Books
of General Interest.

1965, Educational Data Sciences,
Fairfield, NJ.
Providing Computerized Accounting
and Record-Keeping Systems.

1978, Trousimis Research Corp.,
Rockville, MD.
Chemicals for Electron Microscopy.

1979, Stanley H. Kaplan,
New York, NY.
Educational Services.

1976, Environmental Equipment Leasing Co., Fort Collins, CO. Leasing of Environmental Equipment.

1978, City of Kansas City, Kansas City, MO. Zoological Society.

1975, Metro-Goldwyn-Mayer, Inc., Culver City, CA. Education and Entertainment.

1961, Deere and Co.,
Moline, IL.
Agricultural Equipment and Parts.

1962, Akron Catheter, Inc.,
Akron, OH.
Catheters.

1963, Gryphon Corp.,
Burbank, CA.
Motion Picture Film Squeegees.

1973, Agro Land and Cattle Co.,
Tucson, AZ.
Butchered Beef.

1974, Merrill Lynch & Co., Inc.,
New York, NY.
Financial Services.

1976, Pennzoil Co.,
Oil City, PA.
Motor Oils, Lubricants,
Greases, and Solvents.

1974, The W. H. Henry Co.,
Huntington Park, CA.
Adhesives.

1970, Teledyne Industries, Inc.,
Los Angeles, CA.
Engines and Motors for
Land Vehicles.

**1968, Universal Chemicals
and Coating, Inc.,**
Elk Grove Village, IL.
Protective and Decorative Coatings.

1960, The Easterling Co.,
Chicago, IL.
China Tableware.

1972, Art-On Designs, Inc.,
West Bloomfield, MI.
Transfer Paper.

1966, Woorich Corp.,
Woolrich, PA.
Men's and Women's Sportswear,
Woolen Fabrics, Blankets, and
Home Furnishings.

1977, Moto-X-Fox, Inc.,
Campbell, CA.
Lubricants and Fuels.

1976, The DeLeone Corp.,
Santa Clara, CA.
Printed Material.

1968, Federal-Mogul Corp.,
Southfield, MI.
Bearing and Sleeve-Type Bearings.

1962, Carole Accessories, Los Angeles, CA. Real and Costume Jewelry Items.

TRANSPORTATION

KING

1937, Julius J. Stern,
Chicago, IL.
Veneers, Plywood Boards
and Panels, Technical Plywood,
and Composition Boards.

1938, Stetson China Co. Inc.,
Chicago, IL.
China Tableware.

**1920, Griswold Seed
& Nursery Co.,**
Lincoln, NE.
Flower, Vegetable, and Field Seeds.

1928, Sinclair,
New York, NY
Gasoline.

1931, Osborn Paper Co.,
Marion, IN.
Writing Tablets and Pencil Tablets.

**1929, Gager Lime
Manufacturing Co.,**
Sherwood and Chattanooga, TN.
Slaked Lime in Powdered Form.

**1924, The Hi-Flier
Manufacturing Co.,**
Decatur, IL.
Kites.

**1936, Dornier-Metalbau
GmbH,**
Friedrichshafen-am-Bodensee,
Germany.
Aeroplanes and Structural
Parts of Aeroplanes.

1938, Armand Weill & Co.,
Territory of Hawaii.
Men's and Boy's Dress,
Negligee, Hosiery, Pajamas,
and Leather Fabrics.

1938, Gerson Goodman Tutelman Co., Philadelphia, PA. Men's and Boy's Dress Shirts.

1928, Tuf Nut Garment Mfg. Co., Little Rock, AR. Men's and Boys' Negligee Shirts, Trousers, and Coats.

1935, North American Aviation, Inc., Dunford, MD. Airplanes.

1938, Connell Bros. Co. Inc.,
San Francisco, CA.
Flour; Fresh Grapes, Apples,
Pears, Plums, Oranges, and Lemons;
and Canned Fish.

1924, Multiplex Manufacturing Co.,
Berwick, PA.
Pistons for Engines.

1920, Volney W. Mason & Co. Inc.,
Providence, RI.
Hoisting Machinery.

1931, Chicago Roller Skate Co.,
Chicago, IL.
Roller Skates.

1937, Douglas Aircraft Co. Inc.,
Santa Monica, CA.
Airplanes and Structural Parts.

1931, Chicago Roller Skate Co.,
Chicago, IL.
Roller Skates.

1934, Stockton Oil Co.,
Stockton, CA.
Gasoline.

1935, Kronos Titan, A/S,
Fredrikstad, Norway.
Paint Pigments, Paste Paints,
and Ready Mixed Paints.

1928, George R. Burrows, Inc.,
New York, NY.
Tarpaulins, Particularly Tarpaulins
Suitable for Use as Coverings
for All Manner of Boats,
Trucks, or Merchandise.

1925, The Wilcox-Hayes Co.,
Portland, OR.
Wheat Flour.

1933, O'Hara Bros. Co. Inc.,
Boston, MA.
Fresh Fish Fillets,
Frozen Fish Fillets.

1925, Washburn Crosby Co.,
Minneapolis, MN.
Wheat Flour.

1937, Houston Milling Co.,
Houston, TX.
Wheat Flour.

1938, Coffee Sales Co.,
Cedar Rapids, IA.
Coffee.

1932, Wells-Lamont-Smith Corp.,
Minneapolis, MN.
Work Gloves of Fabric
and Combined Fabric Leather.

1934, Kroll Engineering Associates,
New York, NY.
Apparatus for Elevating
a Motor Vehicle Chassis.

**1936, Safety Steering
Stabilizer Co.,**
Pittsburgh, PA.
Automobile Steering Stabilizers.

1923, Auto Truck Equipment Co.,
Pittsburgh, PA.
Cabs, Trucks, Vans, Wood
and Metal Bodies, Special Bodies,
Stakes, Covers, and Sideboards.

Woody Pirtle
PIRTLE DESIGN INC.

My first connection to symbols branding products in our society dates back to the early fifties, when I was a young boy. I remember having an obsessive fascination with the odd bird on the Kiwi Shoe Polish tin, and I was always flexing my bicep when I saw the Arm and Hammer Baking Soda trademark. I also loved the Quaker Oats Pilgrim and the RCA Dog listening to his master's voice.

That early fascination became obsession as I grew older and my view of the world became more expansive. By the time I was in college, in the early sixties, I had become familiar with the work of many accomplished designers.

By the mid-sixties I was enthusiastically studying books on design and marveling at the latest work from Push Pin Studios, Chermayeff and Geismar, Saul Bass, Herb Lubalin, Tom Carnase, and of course, Paul Rand.

One of the first books I was fortunate enough to get my hands on was Paul Theobald's *Trademark Design*, which was published in 1952. This volume is a treasure trove of essays and examples of well-conceived symbols, logotypes, expansive design programs, and more—by iconic masters like Herbert Bayer, Alvin Lustig, Paul Rand, Will Burtin, H. Creston Doner, and others—as well as exemplary work by Raymond Lowey, Louis Danziger, Henry Dreyfuss, A. M. Cassandre, William Golden, Herbert Matter, Lucien Bernhard, and W. A. Dwiggins, to name a few.

I consider Theobald's book to be one of the key building blocks that comprises my foundation in strategic identity design.

I hope that what these masters have taught me and my generation makes them proud of the legacy they have left for countless generations to come.

I'm proud to be a contemporary link in this continuum.

1982, Dallas Opera.

1992, Advanced Surgical.

2001, Delta Faucets.

2001, Brown-Forman.

2003, Crossroads Films.

2004, Brooklyn Ballet.

2004, High Falls Mercantile.

1991, Fine Line Features.

1975, Mr. and Mrs. Aubrey Hair.

1946, Republic Aviation Corp., Farmingdale, NY. Airplanes and Parts Thereof.

1947, The American Oil Co., Baltimore, MD. Gasoline.

1958, Northrop Aircraft, Inc.,
Bevery Hills, CA.
Manned Aircraft,
Missiles, and Drones.

**1947, Cornell Research
Foundation,**
Buffalo, NY.
Models for Comparison
and Study for Technical Use.

1940, The Stouse Adler Co.,
New York, NY.
Men's Undergarments.

1954, North Central Airlines, Inc.,
Minneapolis, MN.
Air Transportation of Persons,
Property, and Mail.

1948, American Airlines, Inc.,
New York, NY.
Air Transport of Passengers
and Freight.

1948, Eastern Air Lines, Inc.,
New York, NY.
Air Transportation of Persons,
Property, and Mail.

1956, Delta Air Lines, Inc.,
Atlanta, GA.
Transportation of Passengers,
Mail, and Express.

1951, Piasecki Helicopter Corp.,
Morton, PA.
Helicopters.

**1956, Standard Oil
Co. of California,**
San Francisco, CA.
Cleaning Compounds
for Household, Professional,
and Commercial Use.

1947, Lockheed Aircraft Corp.,
Burbank, CA.
Airplanes and Structural
Parts Thereof.

1946, Bell Aircraft Corp.,
Wheatfield, NY.
Helicopters and Structural
Parts Thereof.

1956, Western Airlines,
Los Angeles, CA.
Transportation of Passengers,
Mail, and Express.

1955, North American Aviation, Inc., Los Angeles, CA. Rocket Engines and Components Thereof.

1948, Nogero Manufacturing Co., Portland, OR. Detergent and Non-Abrasive Cleaning Preparation.

1947, Standard Oil Company of California, San Francisco, CA. Rust Preventatives and Inhibitors.

1948, Airway Fruit & Vegetable Co., Inc., Baltimore, MD. Fresh Vegetables.

1946, Continental Aviation and Engineering Corp., Detroit, MI. Airplane Propellers and Parts Thereof.

1935, Lubri-Zol Corp.,
Wickliffe, OH.
Gasoline and Chemically Treated
Lubricating Compositions.

1930, Five Minute Home Cleaner Co.,
Chicago, IL.
Dry Cleaner.

1931, Charles L. Haber,
New York, NY.
Locks and Keys.

1938, Garner-Tarkenton,
Wilson, NC.
Non-Alcoholic Soda
Fountain Beverage.

1935, Hahlo & Solomon Inc.,
New York, NY.
Men's and Women's Clothing.

1934, The Heil Co.,
Milwaukee, WI.
Boilers and Furnaces
for Building Heating Purposes.

1925, Bay State Milling Co.,
Helena, MN.
Wheat Flour.

1935, G. Krueger Brewing Co.,
Newark, NJ.
Beer and Ale.

1930, Philadelphia Quartz Co.,
Philadelphia, PA.
Silicate of Soda.

1936, Richmond Radiator Co., Inc., Uniontown, PA. Bath Tubs, Lavatories, Sinks, and Laundry Trays.

My Papa's Leg

It's a "Universal"

1927, Universal Artificial Limb & Supply Co., Inc., Washington, D.C. Artificial Limbs.

1939, A. B. Cook,
Los Angeles, CA.
Non-Alcoholic Beverages.

1934, Peppy Boy Noodle Co.,
Elwood City, PA.
Noodles.

1931, Lucas Manufacturing Co.,
Toledo, OH.
Vehicle Heaters and Parts Thereof.

1928, Cremo Pop Corp.,
New York, NY.
Chocolate Coating for Ice Cream.

1930, Northern Illinois Cereal Co.,
Lockport, IL.
Grits.

1930, Evansville Packing Co.,
Evansville, ID.
Prepared, Smoked, and Dried Beef.

Clive Piercy
AIR CONDITIONED

I was 12 years old when I first became interested in graphic design. I saw the cover of The Beatles' *Sgt. Pepper's Lonely Hearts Club Band* and realized I wanted to do that for a living . . . whatever THAT was. The bread and butter—for some, the champagne and foie gras—for nearly all of us in this industry is the design of logos and trademarks. There's something magical about looking at a logo, liking it for its simple grace, beauty, or purely aesthetic form, then looking again and saying "Oh, yes, I get it. How clever." For me I have always loved the work of the '60s pioneer firm Fletcher/Forbes/Gill and its evolution into today's Pentagram. The timeless qualities in their best work is something I strive to achieve in mine. Ironically, the more sophisticated your eye and taste levels become as a designer, it tends to be the case that you have a greater affection for the types of logos and trademarks that give off a charming naivety, things that appear to have not been designed by a professional designer at all, but born out of necessity and good common sense. It's the same with food. Asked to pick a final great meal, most of us would forego the aforementioned champers and foie gras in favor of a meal that evokes a time and place when we were most happy, invariably something closer to home. That's what we like, too, about the best logos and trademarks and the companies they represent. Having said all that, and putting my designer hat back on, here's a list, in no particular order, of my Top Ten logo trademarks of all time.

Coca-Cola. Hate the drink, love the logo. Designer unknown, I think.
Plessy. Pentagram. Something very satisfying about that squiggly line.
Apple. Robert Janoff. Naturally.
The Olympic Rings. I wish I'd done that one.
The Dubonnet Man. Cassandre, enough said. BEST.
Chermayeff & Geismar. Simple. Very satisfying.
The London Underground. Edward Johnston. Looks easy, and still looks great.
Penguin Books. Edward Young and Jan Tschihold. This one and the Underground one evoke the same affection in me . . . something to do with childhood . . .
ABC. Paul Rand. Thank you, Mr. Rand.
Paul Smith. I love that effortless script.

2008, Alice Supply Co.

1998, Urban Epicuria.

2004, Distributed
Art Publishers.

2005, DNA.

1995, Evans Foden.

1999, Father's Office.

2002, Primary Color.

2006, Roxy.

2000, Stimmüng.

1937, Philadelphia Quartz Co., Philadelphia, PA. Silicate of Soda.

1938, Axton-Fisher Tobacco Co., Louisville, KY. Cigarettes.

1939, Basic Foods, Inc., Jersey City, NJ. Icing for Cakes and Cookies.

1938, Metalmen, Inc., Detroit, MI. Automobile Body and Fender Metal Working Tools.

1935, Esquire, Inc., Chicago, IL. Publications.

1935, RCA Manufacturing Co., Inc., Camden, NJ. Radio and Television Receiving Sets.

1939, Little Beaver, Inc.,
Cleveland, OH.
Comic Drawings Published
in a Series in Daily
and Sunday Newspapers.

1935, Tiona Petroleum Co.,
Philadelphia, PA.
Lubricating Oils, Particularly
for Motors, Tractors, and Trucks.

1920, Frederick F. Brinker,
Peoria, IL.
Canned Adhesive Rubber.

1925, Pioneer Paper Co.,
Los Angeles, CA.
Composition Ready Prepared
Roofings, Building Papers,
Insulating Papers, Flashing
Compound, Lap Cement,
and Chip Board.

1927, W. P. Fuller & Co.,
San Francisco, CA.
Sheet and Plate Glass, Wire Ribbed
Glass, and Wire Corrugated Glass.

1937, Albers Bros. Milling Co.,
Portland, OR.
Corn Flakes.

1935, Shawmut Products Co.,
New York, NY.
Electric Storage Batteries.

1920, Pocahontas Braid Corp.,
New York, NY.
Braid–Stitching, Elastic, Cord Edge,
Cords, Lace, Seam-Binding,
Fringe, Tassels, Rag-Tail Braid,
and Pig-Tail Braid.

**1935, Winter Haven Fruit
Sales Corp.,**
Winter Haven, FL.
Fresh Citrus Fruits—
Namely, Oranges, Grapefruits,
and Tangerines.

1938, The Keefe Packing Co.,
Arkansas City, Kansas.
Barbecue Ham.

1937, Wilson Brothers,
Chicago, IL.
Men's Neckties.

1935, Goldblatt Bros. Inc.,
Chicago, IL.
Beer.

1930, Western Garment Mfg. Co.,
Wichita Falls, TX.
Boys' Pants, Boys' Shirts,
and Boys' Play Suits.

1927, The Stroh Products Co.,
Detroit, MI.
Malt Syrup.

1925, Pioneer Cotton Mills,
Guthrie, OK.
Cotton Duck.

1936, Hecker-H-O Co., Inc.,
Buffalo, NY.
Cereal Food Products—
Namely, Toasted Wheat.

1939, Chesapeake Camp Corp.,
Franklin, VA.
Kraft Paper.

1937, John M. Wilson Feed Mills,
Meridian, MS.
Horse and Mule Feed.

1975, The Love Co., Sioux Falls, SD. All-Purpose Cleaning Preparations.

1935, American Murex Corp., New York, NY. Welding Electrodes.

1953, M. Hohner, Inc.,
New York, NY.
Harmonicas.

**1951, The Brunswick-Balke-
Collender Co.,**
Chicago, IL.
Bowling Score Sheets and Pencils.

1952, Kurt Orban Co.,
New York, NY.
Twist Grill Grinding Machines.

1955 Mid-Co Photo Service,
Wichita, Kansas.
Packaged Photographs.

**1951, The Brunswick-Balke-
Collender Co.,**
Chicago, IL.
Billiard Equipment.

1955, Runnymede Mills, Inc.,
Tarboro, NC.
Boys' and Misses' Hosiery.

1955, The O-P Craft Company, Inc.,
Sandusky, OH.
Household Decoration Kits.

1957, Ferno Manufacturing Co.,
Circleville, OH.
Ambulance Cots
and Morticians' Carts.

1953, Patcraft, Inc.,
Dalton, GA.
Cotton Rugs and Carpets.

1940, Spaulding-Moss Co.,
Boston, MA.
Photo and Litho Prints.

1949, Alfred A. Anthony,
New York, NY.
Toys.

**1952, Superior Paint
and Varnish Corp.,**
Chicago, IL.
Paint, Varnish, and Enamel.

1949, Sterling Bolt Co.,
Chicago, IL.
Bolts, Nuts, Screws, and Rivets.

1949, Doubleday & Company, Inc.,
Garden City, NY.
Books.

1948, Atlas Boxmakers, Inc.,
Chicago, IL.
Packing and Shipping Boxes.

1954, Little Beaver Industries Inc.,
Willoughby, OH.
Shop Hammers.

1947, American Tag Co.,
Chicago, IL.
Printed Tags, Labels, and Tickets.

1954, Kraft Food Co.,
Chicago, IL.
Candy.

**1957, Federal Stamping
and Manufacturing Co.,**
Minneapolis, MN.
Metal Stamping Service.

1945, International Plastic Corp.,
Morristown, NJ.
Paper and Cellulose
Adhesive Tapes.

**1957, National Rural Electric
Cooperative Association,**
Washington, D.C.
Promotion Materials
for Affiliated Companies.

1947, Ely & Walker Dry Goods Co.,
St. Louis, MO.
Textile Piece Goods.

1946, The Safford Co.,
Tryon, NC.
Washing Compounds.

**1950, Topper Undergarment
Company, Inc.,**
New York, NY.
Juniors' and Little Misses' Slips,
Panties, and Nightgowns.

Mr. Controls

1954, Robertshaw-Fulton Controls Co., Greensburg, PA. Main and Pilot Burner Gas Valves.

1953, National Tailoring Co.,
Chicago, IL.
Custom-Made Men's Wear.

1945, Ludwig Scherk, Inc.,
New York, NY.
After-Shave Lotion.

1952, Bartolomeo Pio, Inc.,
Philadelphia, PA.
Wines.

1948, S. Rudofker's Sons, Inc.,
Philadelphia, PA.
Boys' and Men's Clothing.

1947, Allen B. Wrisley Co.,
Chicago, IL.
Perfume.

1940, Mr. Newport, Inc.,
Chicago, IL.
Non-Alcoholic Maltless Beverages.

1954, The Paul Bunyan Bait Co.,
Minneapolis, MN.
Fishing Gear.

**1953, Authentic Furniture
Products, Inc.,**
Los Angeles, CA.
Milk Stools, Tables, and Chairs.

1955, Schalk Chemical Co.,
Los Angeles, CA.
Tile Adhesive.

1953, Braunstein Freres, Inc.,
New York, NY.
Cigarette Paper.

1950, William Boyd,
Beverly Hills, CA.
Children's Clothing.

1945, Wynne Precision Co.,
Griffin, GA.
Fishing Tackle.

**1952, Matthews Thrifty Lady
Super Markets,**
Atlanta, GA.
Packaged Dried Beans.

1955, R. Kelly Office Service, Inc.,
Detroit, MI.
Equipment and Furnishings
for Temporary Offices.

1945, Revoc, Inc.,
New York, NY.
Cigars, Cigarettes, Pipe
and Chewing Tobacco.

1952, Post-Hall Syndicate, Inc., New York, NY. Comic Strip.

1940, Minnesota Macaroni Co., St. Paul, MN. Macaroni, Spaghetti, and Egg Noodles.

1949, RCA Service Co., Inc., Camden, NJ. Theater Sound Equipment.

1946, H.J. Hueller Manufacturing Co.,
Brooklyn, NY.
Oil Burner Units.

1946, Engineering Manufacturing Co.,
Sheboygan, WI.
Drafting Equipment.

1940, Lily-Tulip Corp.,
New York, NY.
Paper Cups and Containers.

1940, Cortland Line Co., Inc.,
Cortland, NY.
Fishing Lines.

1950, The Cooper Alloy Foundry Co.,
Hillside, NJ.
Pipe Fitting and Valves.

1958, The Perry Knitting Co.,
Perry, NY.
Infants' and Children's Sleepers.

1957, Altec Lansing Corp., Beverly Hills, CA. Speakers, Tuners, and Amplifiers.

1946, Scott & Williams, Inc., Strafford, NH. Hosiery for Men, Women, and Children.

Sharon Werner
WERNER DESIGN WERKS, INC.

A small glimpse of our history.

From as far back as I can remember I've been interested in and inspired by graphic design history. Trademarks are merely a small glimpse of that history. At its core a trademark was just that, a *mark* that symbolized a *trade* or product. It was honest and simple and said everything in one small spot illustration. Nearly every company from large corporations to small mom-and-pop shops had a trademark of some sort. Thought and care went into saying something tangible and real about the person and the product or service.

I was coming out of college and just starting at Duffy Design Group in the mid-eighties when floating triangles, random lines, and circles were the style of the moment. But I admired the early trademarks, every one created and drawn with a human hand. Charming and personable in their imperfections: soft corners, rough edges, slightly inconsistent line weight, and an ever so slightly off balance character led to an aesthetic quality that is much more difficult to capture digitally. There was honesty and a personality that I felt was lacking in the then current work.

I spent hours, diligently photocopying vintage yellow pages from the storage stacks of the library, and scouring antique stores for paper ephemera, trying to build a collection of inspirational trademarks. In 1986 I stumbled upon a copy of *Trademarks of the '20s and '30s*; at last I had found my holy grail. The book was affordable, even to an intern.

Over the years I've intently studied these trademarks of the early twentieth century. Of course there were many times I was tempted to simply lift the design and re-use it as is for a new client. It was so perfectly imperfect, how could I ever do something better? But I refrained; at least I hope I did. Instead I began to really see that it was the honesty and the quality of the drawing as well as the wit and humor that I found so appealing in the trademarks. They were made by people, for people.

antenna

2009, Antenna.

1994, Ripsaw Photography.

1995, Fresh Werks.

**2000, Mrs. Meyer's
Clean Day.**

2003, GrandConnect.

1999, Skwish Classic.

**1992, Werner Design
Werks, Inc.**

2004, TV by Girls.

2007, Outdoor LAB.

1970, R. R. Donnelley & Sons Co.,
Chicago, IL.
Printing Services.

1964, The American Tobacco Co.,
New York, NY.
Cigarettes.

1964, The Rath Packing Co.,
Waterloo, IA.
Refrigerated Meats
and Prepared Meat Products.

**1967, Buffalo Bill's
Steak Village, Inc.,**
Los Angeles, CA.
Restaurant Services.

1974, 20th Century Club, Inc.,
Coconut Grove, FL.
Social Club Services.

1978, Dew Corp.,
Tulsa, OK.
Restaurant Services.

1966, Sarong, Inc.,
Dover, DE.
Body Powder.

**1960, Coast Ballet Manufacturing
Company, Inc.,**
Hollywood, CA.
Women's Shoes.

**1972, Coast Ballet
Manufacturing Company, Inc.,**
Hollywood, CA.
Square Dance and Ballet Shoes.

1960, First Federal Savings and Loan Association of Kansas City,
Kansas City, MO.
Financial Services.

1960, Artistic Card Publishing Co.,
Elmira, NY.
Greeting Cards.

1960, National Corporation Service, Inc.,
New Orleans, LA.
Furnishes Uniformed Guards, Watchmen, and Patrol Services.

1963, Variety Homes, Inc.,
Newington, CT.
Shell Homes and Components.

1962, Allprints Photo, Inc.,
Mansfield, OH.
Film Processing.

1964, Walker Manufacturing Co.,
Racine, WA.
Exhaust System Parts.

1968, Banco Credito y Ahorro Ponceno.,
Ponce, Puerto Rico.
Banking Services.

1974, The Baxter Corp.,
Paterson, NJ.
Paper Goods and Printed Matter.

1962, Whiring-Plover Paper Co.,
Stevens Point, WI.
Fine Paper and Printers' Stock.

1960, The Cracker Jack Co., Chicago, IL. Marshmallows.

1964, Lawrence Children's Underwear Company, Inc., New York, NY. Children's Wear.

1970, Monique's School of Modeling and Finishing, South Bend, IN. Instruction and Training of Models.

1970, Mediprod Laboratories, Inc., Selma, AL. Spray Hair Cream for Men.

1960, St. Regis Paper Co.,
New York, NY.
Paperboard Cartons.

1965, Fabmagic, Inc.,
Santa Ana, CA.
Rug Shampoo.

1966, Cool-It, Inc.,
Chicago, IL.
Aftershave Lotion.

1960, British West India Airways,
New York, NY.
Transportation, Planning,
and Tour Services.

1964, The Dow Chemical Co.,
Midland, MI.
Dry Cleaning Products.

**1960, Decatur Federal Savings
and Loan Association,**
Decatur, GA.
Savings and Loan Services.

1969, The Proctor & Gamble Co.,
Cincinnati, OH.
Shampoo.

1967, KAS Manufacturing Co.,
New York, NY.
Electrically Operated Facial Sauna.

1970, Sebastian's International Inc.,
Spokane, WA.
Restaurant and Tavern Services.

1968, De Leon Cosmetics Co., Inc.,
Omaha, NE.
Makeup.

1968, Think Thin International,
Long Beach, CA.
Diet Systems and Diet Products.

1978, Lorelle,
Seattle, WA.
Costume Jewelry
Sold at Home Parties.

1963, T-N-T Food Products, Inc., Lawrence, KS. Unpopped Popcorn.

1962, Rosebud Lumber Co.,
Rosebud, OR.
Plywood.

1970, Graphic, Inc.,
Crystal, MN.
Printing Services.

1962, American Greetings Corp.,
Cleveland, OH.
Greeting Cards.

1965, Dermik Pharmaceutical Co.,
Syosset, NY.
Benzoyl Peroxide and Calcium
Phosphate for Use in Lotions.

1966, Mr. Mod Shop, Inc.,
New Orleans, LA.
Men's Cologne.

1960, Stanley Greetings, Inc.,
Dayton, OH.
Greeting Cards.

1974, Pontchartrain State Bank,
Metairie, LA.
Banking Services.

1976, The Gillette Co.,
Boston, MA.
Smoke Detectors.

1976, Stihl, Inc.,
Virginia Beach, VA.
Chain Saws.

1960, The Reynolds & Reynolds Co.,
Dayton, OH.
Accounting Services.

1969, Oklahoma City Tractor Co.,
Oklahoma City, OK.
Equipment Trailers.

1968, Ashworth Brothers, Inc.,
Fall River, MA.
Metal and Hybrid Conveyor Belting.

**1960, Liberty Fabrics
of New York, Inc.,**
New York, NY.
Lace.

1966, Red Devil, Inc.,
Union, NJ.
Hardware and Plumbing Supplies.

**1977, The Straw Hat
Restaurant Corp.,**
Dublin, CA.
Restaurant Services.

1978, Hercules Service Corp., Johnstown, PA. Car and Truck Rustproofing Services.

1978, Ace Designing Co., San Francisco, CA. Provides Temporary Technical Personnel.

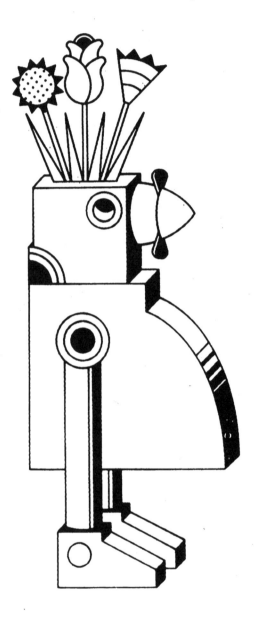

1978, Brooklyn Institute of Arts and Sciences, Brooklyn, NY. Paper Goods and Printed Matter.

1962, Pacific Metals Co., San Francisco, CA. Welding Materials.

CIRCLES AND SHAPES

1938, R.M. Hollingshead Corp.,
Camden, NJ.
Varnish, Stains, Fillers, Lacquers,
Ready Mixed Paints, Enamels,
and Coatings.

1936, Atlas Tack Corp.,
Fairhaven, MA.
Nails and Tacks.

1936, National Sulphur Co. Inc.,
New York, NY.
Flowers of Sulphur.

1920, Johnson Oil Refining Co.,
Chicago Heights, IL.
Petroleum, Gasoline, Kerosene,
Naphtha, Lubricating Oils, Distillate,
and Lubricating Greases.

1938, Sigmund W. Zabienek,
Chelsea, MA.
Miniature Hockey Rink Game.

1929, Sklaroff Brothers,
Philadelphia, PA.
Hosiery.

1931, The Tabulating Machine Co., New York, NY. For Card Controlled Tabulating Machines, Card Punching Machines, Card Sorting Machines, and Card Duplicating Machines.

1937, Natural Set Up Sales Corp.,
St. Louis, MO.
Carbonated Soft Drinks
with Lemon Flavor Predominating.

1925, Barrows Optical Corp.,
Providence, RI.
Ophthalmic Mountings.

1934, Delta Electric Co.,
Marion, IN.
Electric Hand Lanterns, Electric
Bicycle Lamps, Electric Vehicle
Lamps, and Electric Horns.

1936, Mayer-Stern, Inc.,
Allentown, IN.
Men's and Women's Polo
and Sport Shirts.

1937, The Enns Milling Co.,
Inman, KS.
Wheat Flour and Self-Rising
Wheat Flour.

1920, The Acme Mills,
Hopkinsville, KY.
Self-Rising Wheat Flour.

1926, J.E. Rhoads & Sons,
Philadelphia, PA.
Belt Preserver and Dressing
and Liquid Belt Preserver.

1935, The Liquid Carbonic Corp.,
Chicago, IL
Solid Carbon Dioxide.

**1925, Walter M. Steppacher
& Bro. Inc.,**
Philadelphia, PA.
Dress, Negligee, Night,
or Work Shirts, Pajamas,
and Men's Textile Underwear.

**1925, Mackie Pine Oil
Specialty Co. Inc.,**
Covington, LA.
Disinfectant and Deodorant
Used in the Bath.

1925, Skelly Oil Co.,
Tulsa, OK.
Natural Gasoline, Motor Gasoline,
Kerosene, Distillate, Gas Oil,
and Industrial Lubricants.

1929, Milton Bradley Co.,
Springfield, MA.
Checkerboards.

Sam Potts
SAM POTTS INC.

My favorite of all the logos I've ever designed was for a film production company called Antidote Films. It was just a lowercase "z" followed by a period. I thought it was just right on—the initial of "Antidote" was "A" and an antidote is a kind of opposite, so the antidote of "A" would be "Z" (I made it lowercase to drive the point home). Simple in form, pure in idea—it was everything a logo needed to be. But still: it was bad.

I was a first-year design student.

So where did I fail? After all, it's not wrong to aim for a logo that reduces an idea to its most essential elements, not wrong for the ultimate design to embody some core element or quality of the thing it stands for. It worked great in black and white at any size. It was even modular—any typeface would work—and a whole system could be generated from the idea of initials for everything. But still: bad.

The problem was, of course, no one got it. Not the designers and not the non-designers I showed it to. And everyone to whom I've described this logo has had the same general reaction: they roll their eyes. My z. was both impossible to understand and totally obvious. That's not entirely easy to pull off, but it's not good design, either.

Being quickly and completely understood is really the only job a logo has. That's the whole discipline, all of what makes a logo work and what makes designing them so difficult. A logo doesn't have to carry any actual information, doesn't have to prove a point or tell you anything that you didn't already know. And yet that's what it does—because it has to be the thing that stands for everything else. It has to embody the qualities of its referent and also evoke them in their absence. Furthermore, the really good logos do all this without us even knowing it's happening. We understand a good logo without having to understand it at all.

When I design a logo, I try for something that formally holds together in and of itself, with a self-contained force that makes it feel whole. I don't generally make logos that are pictures of things. Rather, I try to make logos that through concept or typography or arrangement will somehow wave their arms and point in the direction of what you are supposed to understand about it. So that, with luck, you get it without getting it.

2006, Pangloss Films.

2002, AIX Restaurant.

2005, IFC Center.

2004, They Might Be Giants.

2004, 826 NYC.

2008, Jonathan Coulton,
Musician.

2000, Antidote Films.

2006, FR.OG Restaurant.

2004, Believer Books.

1936, Cornelius Publications, Inc., Indianapolis, IN. Periodical Published at Regular Intervals.

1938, Container Corp. of America,
Chicago, IL.
Wood Pulp.

1925, Texas Portland Cement Co.,
Dallas, TX.
Portland Cement.

1938, Olden Minerals, Inc.,
Los Angeles, CA.
Pharmaceutical Preparations
Used in Mineral Baths for Inducing
Sleep, Promoting Circulation
of the Blood, Reducing Weight,
and Alleviating Pains.

1927, Household Guide Corp.,
New York, NY.
Publication Issued Monthly.

1937, Funk Bros. Seed Co. Inc.,
Chicago, IL.
Seeds, Seed Grains.

**1936, Republic Electric
Manufacturing Co.,**
Davenport, IA.
Radio Receiving Sets, Generators,
and Storage Batteries.

1935, Stanley P. Brown,
Mission, TX.
Fresh Citrus Fruits.

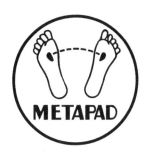

1929, Heywood Boot & Shoe Co.,
Worcester, MA.
Leather Boots and Shoes.

1925, Northern Pacific Railway Co.,
St. Paul, MN.
Booklets, Circulars, and Pamphlets.

1957, Personal Shoe Co.,
Haverhill, MA.
Molding Kits for Shoes.

1948, W.W. MacGruder, Inc.,
Denver, CO.
Passenger Airline Transportation.

1957, J. Warren Bowman,
St. Petersburg, FL.
Snacks Formed of Grain
and Other Materials.

**1958, Moore's Time-Saving
Equipment, Inc.,**
Indianapolis, IN.
Rug-Cleaning Equipment.

1948, Louis G. Cowan, Inc.,
New York, NY.
Radio Program Series
on Mystery Dramas.

1955, Whitin Machine Works,
Whitinsville, MA.
Direct-Image Paper Plates
for Offset Duplication.

1951, Fred W. Albertson,
Washington, D.C.
Radio and Wire Teletypewriters.

1953, Signode Steel Strapping Co.,
Chicago, IL.
Load-Retaining Doors.

1956, Borg-Warner Corp.,
Chicago, IL.
Overdrives, Brakes,
and Parts Thereof.

1940, Schering & Glatz, Inc.,
Bloomfield, NJ.
Rectal Suppositories.

1943, William R. Warner & Co.,
New York, NY.
Medicinal Preparations Indicated
in the Treatment of Constipation,
Neuralgia, and Headaches.

1946, Murray Silverstein,
Brooklyn, NY.
Ladies' Undergarments.

1946, Waldorf Paper Products Co., St. Paul, MN. Corrugated Paper Board.

1947, Robert Gair Co., New York, NY. Folding Paperboard Cartons and Corrugated Fiberboard Shipping Boxes.

1956, General Motors Corp.,
Detroit, MI.
Washing, Drying,
and Ironing Machines.

**1953, Grant Pulley
& Hardware Corp.,**
Flushing, NY.
Mounting Hardware
for Doors and Windows.

1945, E.L. Mustee & Sons,
Cleveland, OH.
Gas Water Heaters.

1956, Beebe Brothers,
Seattle, WA.
Winches.

1942, Shook Bronze Corp.,
Lima, OH.
Busing Metals.

**1947, Water Service
Laboratories, Inc.,**
New York, NY.
Chemical Treatment
of Domestic Water.

Eric Strohl
STROHL

Growing up in rural North Carolina, I couldn't have been further from the slicked-up world of costly brand and marketing campaigns. With agriculture as the primary industry, we opted to keep our brands conservative and respectable. My first memories were of painted logos adorning delivery trucks on my early morning rides to school—Hanes Textiles, Camel Cigarettes, Cheerwine, and, of course, local favorite Texas Pete Hot Sauce (which was neither from Texas, nor made by anyone named Pete).

All of these marks were simple, direct—utilizing either custom typography, or a memorable icon, mascot, or illustration to make it relatable and memorable. Almost every barbeque stand in the "Camel City" had a pig of some sort as their logo, but it was the subtle differences in execution that defined your brand preference. Did you buy your pulled pork sandwich from the life-size standing hog that was carving up his own body with fork and knife, or from the fancy animated neon piglets that bounded over the flickering type thousands of times nightly? I didn't translate these observations into graphic design until my father became a creative director at AT&T and our home became flooded with pads, pens, and other items emblazoned with the iconic Saul Bass logo. What captivated me was the icon's ability to create the optical illusion of full dimensionality in such a simple two-dimensional rendering.

The trademarks that remain dear to me are similar in that respect, each stripping away layers of finish and unnecessary varnish leaving just the simplest representation intact. I've always been partial to publishing logos because of this. What better test of a trademark than a stamped, single-color image on a slender book spine to convey the entire brand essence of a major publishing house? Knopf, Random House, and Penguin have always been favorites, especially the work by Clarence Hornung.

So what will the future hold for the iconic American trademark? I hope this collection of masterfully crafted marks will inspire future generations of designers to help return simplicity and cleverness to our disappearing craft.

It's what Texas Pete would have wanted.

2004, Harper Collins.

2000, Wilrik Apartments.

2002, Gotham Books.

**2003, Hell's Kitchen
Flea Market.**

2005, Morgan Road Books.

2008, The Designers Accord.

2004, New American Library.

**2004, Bernard's
Market & Cafe.**

2007, 18 Rabbits Granola.

1940, Standard Oil Co. of Calif.,
San Francisco, CA.
Gasoline, Lubricating Oils,
and Greases.

1948, The Cleveland Gypsum Co.,
Cleveland, OH.
Mill Mix Plasters and Mortars.

1954, Coachcraft, Ltd.,
Hollywood, CA.
Automobile Air-Conditioners
and Luggage Carriers.

1953, The Garrett Corp.,
Los Angeles, CA.
Air-Conditioning and Refrigeration.

**1948, Michel & Pfeffer
Iron Works, Inc.,**
San Francisco, CA.
Structural Parts for Steel Buildings.

**1940, The Emerson Electric
Manufacturing Co.,**
St. Louis, MO.
Electric Motor Controls.

1940, Roux Distributing Co.,
New York, NY.
Hair Colorings, Shampoos,
Tints, Bleach, and Bluing.

1949, Electronics Systems Corp.,
Kansas City, MO.
Diminutive Radio Receiving Sets.

1947, West Point Hoisery Co.,
West Point, PA.
Women's Hosiery.

1940, The Sherwin-Williams Co., Cleveland, OH. Paints, Enamels, Lacquers, Fillers, and Pigments.

1946, Delta Color Corp., New York, NY. Ready-Mixed Waterbase Show Card Color.

1940, RKO Pictures, New York, NY. Recorded Sounds and Images on Films Adapted for Reproduction.

1949, Lien Chemical Co.,
Franklin Park, IL.
Insecticide Powders
and Household Disinfectants.

1956, John C. Virden Co.,
Cleveland, OH.
Electric Lighting Fixtures.

1948, Thonet Brothers, Inc.,
New York, NY.
Chairs, Stools, Sofas, and Tables.

1952, Mueller Welt, Inc.,
Chicago, IL.
Contact Lenses.

1952, Shure Brothers, Inc.,
Chicago, IL.
Piezoelectric Instruments
to Measure and Analyze Vibrations.

1953, Menasco Manufacturing Co.,
Burbank, CA.
Aircraft Landing Gear.

1956, Oris Watch Co., Ltd.,
Holstein, Switzerland.
Watches, Clocks, Dials, and Cases.

1947, American Colloid Co.,
Chicago, IL.
Bentonite Clays.

1946, Silvray Co., Inc.,
New York, NY.
Electric Lamps.

1960, Industrial Incomes, Inc.,
Jackson Heights, NY.
Financial Services.

1961, Imperial Household Shipping,
Long Beach, CA.
Shipping Company.

1960, The Globe Steel Abrasive Co.,
Mansfield, OH.
Abrasive Shot and Grit.

1968, Educational Development Corp.,
Palo Alto, CA.
Magazine.

1967, Fairmont Food Co.,
Omaha, NE.
Carbonated Soft Drinks
and Concentrates.

1966, Midland International Corp.,
North Kansas City, MO.
Radio Receivers and Transceivers,
Intercommunication Sets, Batteries,
and Battery Chargers.

1962, Blackwelder Manufacturing Co.,
Rio Vista, CA.
Agricultural Equipment.

1967, Whitman Publishing Co.,
Racine, WI.
Magnifying Lenses.

1969, International Biophysics Corp.,
Fullerton, CA.
Transducers, Electrodes,
and Treated Pads.

**1974, Community Church
of Religious Science,**
Los Angeles, CA.
Religious Educational Books.

1968, Action Plastics Co.,
Los Angeles, CA.
Extruded Plastic Tubing.

1975, The Spinning Wheel,
Blytheville, AR.
Bicycle Parts.

1967, Earl Scheib, Inc., Beverly Hills, CA. Automotive Painting and Associated Services.

1973, AIFS-Delaware, Greenwich, CT. Promoting Foreign Study.

**1961, Publications
Development Corp.,**
New York, NY.
Books.

1969, Mitsubishi Rayon Co., Ltd.,
Tokyo, Japan.
Padding and Stuffing Materials.

**1965, Cowies Educational
Books, Inc.,**
New York, NY.
Reference Books.

1967, Daiwa Corp.,
Gardena, CA.
Fishing Reels and Fishing Rods.

1965, Sunshine Brewing Co.,
Reading, PA.
Beer.

1968, Comfort Glass Corp.,
Miami, FL.
Heat-Reflective Film Products.

1970, The Midnight Sun, Inc.,
Atlanta, GA.
Restaurant Services.

**1969, First National Bank
of Belleville,**
Belleville, IL.
General Banking Services.

1972, Smithsonian Institution,
Washington, D.C.
Museum Services.

1968, The Inn,
Bermuda Dunes, CA.
Hotel/Motel Services.

**1971, Virgin Islands Public
Television System,**
Charlotte Amalie,
St. Thomas, VI.
Educational Television
Broadcasting Services.

1975, Solar Audio Products, Inc.,
Los Angeles, CA.
Speakers and Speaker Systems.

1975, Howmedica, Inc.,
New York, NY.
Pharmaceuticals.

1973, Azteca Corn Products Corp.,
Chicago, IL.
Partially Prepared Mexican Foods.

1964, Optics International Corp.,
Philadelphia, PA.
Headbands and Sun Visors.

1965, The American Tobacco Co.,
New York, NY.
Cigars.

1968, National Airlines, Inc.,
Miami, FL.
Air Transportation of Freight
and Passengers.

1976, Sunhandlers, Inc.,
Cocoa, FL.
Thermal Insulating Films.

Dana Arnett, James Koval, and Curt Schreiber
VSA Partners, Inc.

When asked to contribute work to this publication, I was reminded of the old adage, "You can tell a lot about things by the way they look." These words provide a simple metaphor for how naked and singular a logo is in its purest form. Realistically, logos will always fall prey to the larger forces of public perception and interpretation. Whether we like it or not, the general population remains the most vocal force of acceptance or rejection of a logo.

A number of years ago, I taught an identity course at the university level. I would often remind my students of this simple fact: "symbol" is the root word of Symbolism. I fostered the notion that, beyond the technical and tailored aspects of creating a great graphic mark, the best logos are those which tell a story and inspire a deeper meaning—an intention or explanation that extends far beyond the confines of the expression itself. Perhaps this also explains why creating logos can be such a challenging and stimulating area of work for designers. There's always this wonderful tension at play between artistic form and explicit meaning. Paul Rand explained this dichotomy best when he described logos as "the abstract joining hands with the concrete." Being one of the finest at this craft, his take on corporate identity also validates another theory of mine: strong-willed designers create the best identities. And few were more bold and successful than he was in making a singular image stand for something so much larger.

Like religion and politics, logos symbolize a much deeper identity than any single person or organization could ever represent. And while there will always be fruitful arguments about how good or bad a symbol is, or why a trademark does or doesn't work, by definition identities are partisan. It's not the logo itself that's the source of debate, but the identity of "who" or "what" the logo truly represents that matters in the end.

—Dana Arnett

2008, Chicago 2016.

2008, AGI Chicago.

2009, eQ Journal.

2004, IBM Values.

2001, Cingular.

1997, Jim Cary.

2002, Brunswick.

1988, Playboy.

2003, Thomas Pheasant.

1961, The Paramount Line, Inc.,
Pawtucket, RI.
Greeting Cards.

**1970, The Walter Reade
Organization, Inc.,**
Oakhurst, NJ.
Prints and Publications

1963, Permanent Peace Association,
New York, NY.
Identifies Members of Association.

1969, Sid Galper,
Los Angeles, CA.
Landscape Architecture.

1974, Ralston Purina Co.,
St. Louis, MO.
Recreational Services.

1966, W. A. Benjamin, Inc.,
New York, NY.
Textbooks.

1965, King Foods, Inc.,
Newport, MN.
Frozen Meats.

1963, Philippine Cigar Co.,
San Francisco, CA.
Tobacco Products.

1962, Bilt-Rite Baby Carriage Co.,
Brooklyn, NY.
Doll Carriages.

1962, Stover Plywood Corp.,
New York, NY.
Refinished Plywood Panels
and Plywood Doors.

1963, The Quaker Oats Co.,
Chicago, IL.
Biscuits and Cookies.

1967, The Earl of Hardwicke, Ltd.,
New York, NY.
Drinking and Eating Ware
Made of China.

1963, Crown Paper Box Corp., Indianapolis, IN. Folding and Set-Up Paper Boxes.

1970, The Empress Corp., Los Angeles, CA. Women's and Men's Sports Clothing.

1960, Clairol Inc.,
New York, NY.
Shampoo.

1960, Crown Zellerbach Corp.,
San Francisco, CA.
Lumber and Plywood.

**1964, World's Finest
Chocolate, Inc.,**
Chicago, IL.
Candy.

1964, Master Made Paints, Inc.,
Joplin, MO.
Paints.

1975, V.R. Intimate Apparel, Inc.,
New York, NY.
Women's Clothing.

1960, Imperial Books,
Baltimore, MD.
Series of Books.

1963, Royal of Pittsburgh, Inc.,
Pittsburgh, PA.
Jewelry.

1962, The Fuller Brush Co.,
East Hartford, CT.
Hairbrushes and Clothes Brushes.

1968, Vincent et Vincent,
Washington, D.C.
Beauty Parlor Services.

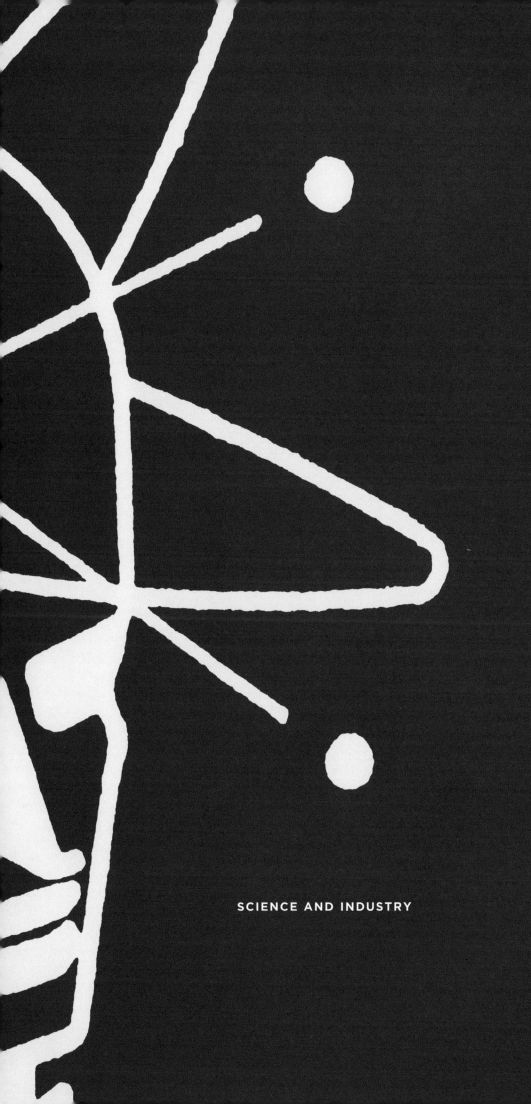

SCIENCE AND INDUSTRY

1956, New Rochelle Manufacturing Co.,
New Rochelle, NY.
Piston Pumps.

1957, Schulmerich Carillons, Inc.,
Sellersville, PA.
Woven Cotton Cloth.

**1958, Automation Institute
of America, Inc.,**
San Francisco, CA.
Classroom Instruction Courses
in Business Automation.

**1956, Cleveland Institute
of Radio Electronics,**
Cleveland, OH.
Pamphlets, Books,
and Other Publications.

1956, Hycon Electronics, Inc.,
Pasadena, CA.
Test Equipment for Televisions.

**1957, Atomic Development
Mutual Fund, Inc.,**
Washington, D.C.
Mutual Funds Investments
for Atomic Science.

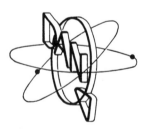

1956, Hycon Electronics, Inc.,
Pasadena, CA.
Test Equipment for Televisions.

1954, The Standard Oil Co.,
Cleveland, OH.
Gasoline.

1956, Growler Alarm Corp.,
New York, NY.
Electrical Fire and Police
Burglar Alarm.

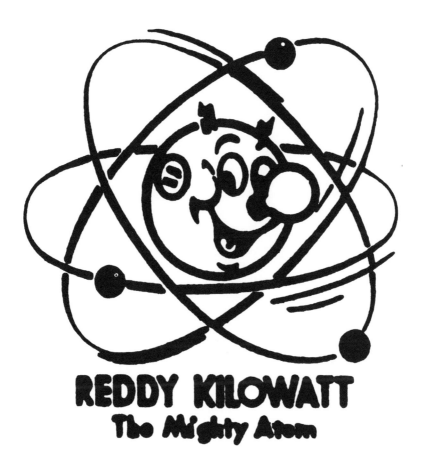

1956, Reddy Kilowatt, Inc., New York, NY. Circulars and Advertising Matter.

Scott Stowell
OPEN

When we're just starting out, many of us designers think that logos need to say and do everything. We get some job in high school or college to make a logo for "Joe's Fancy Pizza" or something like that, and we spend forever trying to get Joe and Fancy and Pizza in there. A lot of clients think the same way—that a logo can say everything they want to say and solve all of their problems. But a logo is just the way you sign your name. What your name means is something else.

The thing is, the most meaningful and memorable symbols don't say or do much of anything. Paul Rand himself said that companies make logos great, not the other way around. Like your signature, all a logo really needs to do is identify who you are and express some hint of what you're about. If people can recognize and remember your logo, you're all set. I'm a big fan of logos anybody can draw. If that drawing is also meaningful (like Rand's UPS logo), even better.

These days logos have to work on TV and Web sites and phones, so they can move and change. But most logos also still have to work on business cards and baseball caps and shipping cartons, so they can't always move and change. And making something work when it's tiny on a screen and making something work when it's embroidered on a hat require pretty much the same things: a good idea, a clear form, some nice type. After that it can move and change all you want.

This is why logos are hard to make. It's also why I love making them. Logos may not need to say and do everything, but getting those hints of meaning in there and making sure they work whenever and wherever they have to are very specific problems to solve. To make your logo, we need to learn about who you are. But by designing your signature, we're helping you figure out who you want to be. So a good logo may not make you great, but it couldn't hurt.

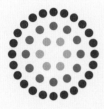

2002, e-Parliament.

1999, Look-Look.

2000, aMedia.

1995, Houghton Mifflin Interactive.

2007, Brooklyn Bridge Park.

2006, National Multiple
Sclerosis Society.

2004, Bravo.

2007, WNYC Radio.

2007, Planet Green.

1953, L. H. Kellog Chemical Co., Minneapolis, MN. Embalming Chemicals and Disinfectants.

1946, North American Phillips Co., Inc.
Dobbs Ferry, NY.
X-Ray Apparatus for Inspection
Tests and Lab Experiments.

1955, Hiresta Laboratories, Inc.,
New York, NY.
Skin Lotion.

1957, Manson Laboratories, Inc.,
Stamford, CT.
Devices to Measure Frequencies.

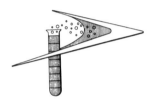

1957, Turco Products, Inc.,
Los Angeles, CA.
Organic Polymer and Non-
Aqueous Solvent Used
as a Protective Coating.

1955, Original Designs Ltd.,
Honolulu, HI.
Design and Construction of
Residential Buildings.

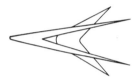

1956, Chrysler Corp.,
Highland Park, MI.
Motor Vehicles
and Their Structural Parts.

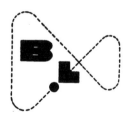

1955, Benson-Lehner Corp.,
Los Angeles, CA.
Equipment to Translate
Various Data.

1956, Lockheed Aircraft Corp.,
Burbank, CA.
Airplanes and Components Thereof.

1957, The Zeller Corp.,
Defiance, OH.
Aircraft Repair.

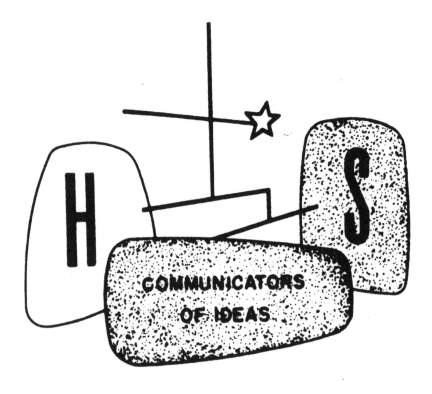

1955, Henry Strauss & Co., Inc., New York, NY. Sales Promotion Booklets, Reports, and Posters.

1953, Isotope Products Ltd., Oakville, Ontario, Canada. Devices for Detecting Radiation.

1953, Rocket Coal Co.,
Barbourville, KY.
Bituminous Coal.

1955, S. Goldberg & Co., Inc.,
Hackensack, NJ.
House Slippers for Men,
Women, and Children.

1952, Space Stamps Co.,
New York, NY.
Pictorial Novelty Stamps.

1950, Price Battery Corp.,
Hamburg, PA.
Storage Batteries.

1955, Harold J. Barnes,
New York, NY.
Space Detective Game.

1947, Good Luck Glove Co.,
Carbondale, IL.
Work Glove Made of Leather
and Cotton Flannel.

1945, Worthington Products Co., Arlington, VA, Insecticides.

1953, Major Distributing Co., Salinas, CA. Fresh Carrots.

Michael Cronan
: : CRONAN : :

What will logos look like in another fifty or one hundred or five hundred years? How will we visualize distinct identities for products or groups of people or alignments of process and collections of services? Will logos serve the same functions in the future?

Just as we look at the history of trademarks and are charmed by logos from the past, it seems inevitable that the vast majority of logos created for today's world will seem nostalgic, even simple-minded when considered in the future.

That eventuality doesn't daunt the designer's continued willingness to try to create something that can achieve a kind of ageless relationship with the idea it represents and to achieve recognition in the culture.

It is a privilege as well as a pleasure to try to capture the vitality and spirit of something and distill it into a word or symbol that memorably communicates a big idea. It is very rewarding to see how a company can effectively succeed and prosper because it adopts the work we create. And when a trade name enters the dictionary or a trademark comes to universally represent an experience, it is a special thing, a joy indeed for the creator of the name or logo.

Perhaps those events contain a tiny kernel of legacy for the designer, although rarely is his or her name attached to the work and recognized by the general public. More likely the joy comes from being at a time and place where something positive and interesting was started, was launched, was born—and even having a small degree of responsibility for its success.

One thing is certain, logos and visual identities adapt and change as culture and technology change. The process began in the dim past and will continue into the future. As long as there is a need to make choices between one religion and another, or one toothpaste and another, there will be the need to create and support names and visual identities to distinguish and identify the available choices. More importantly, as long as great new ideas are coming into reality, there will be talented and dedicated people who will strive to name and create logos for them.

1980, Beethoven.

2003, Founding Fathers.

1992, Walking Man.

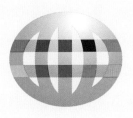

2007, FORA.tv.

1998, TiVo.

2004, The Stem Cell Meeting.

1995, San Francisco
Museum of Modern Art.

2006, Healthy Child
Healthy World.

1983, San Francisco
Symphony.

**1947, Cleveland Institute
of Radio Electronics,**
Cleveland, OH.
School Publications
on Radio Electronics.

1955, Kingston Electronic Corp.,
Cambridge, MA.
Absorption Analyzers.

**1956, Fairchild Engine
and Airplane Corp.,**
Costa Mesa, CA.
Resistance Bridge Indicators
and Balances.

1956, Burtel Corp.,
Redwood City, CA.
Forceps.

1948, Pasadena Research, Inc.,
Pasadena, CA.
Vitamins and Pharmaceuticals.

**1953, Medical Management
Control,**
San Francisco, CA.
Bookkeeping, Accounting,
and General Office Forms
and Ledgers.

**1952, Industrial Engineering
Drafting Co.,**
Brooklyn, NY.
Drawing Industrial Maps
to Specification.

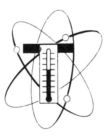

1957, Temptron, Inc.,
Columbus, OH.
Furnaces.

**1953, Whittaker Guernsey
Studio, Inc.,**
Chicago, IL.
Preparation of Artwork
and Advertising Materials.

**1956 Chemionics Engineering
Laboratories, Inc.,**
Wilmington, NC.
Copper Napthenate
Wood Preservative.

1956, United Catalog Publishers, Inc.,
New York, NY.
Publications on Electronics.

1954, Blaupunkt Electronik GmbH,
Berlin-Wimersdorf, West Germany.
Phonographs, Dictating Machines,
and Sound Recording Machines.

1957, Hess & Clark, Inc.,
Ashland, OH.
Poultry, Stock, and Veterinary
Remedies and Medicated
Feed Concentrates.

1947, Adams and Powell, Inc.,
New York, NY.
General Building Contracting Work.

1949, The J. M. Fink Company, Inc.,
New York, NY.
Designing and Installing
Air-Conditioning, Heating,
and Refrigeration Systems.

1948, Pacific Gas Corp.,
New York, NY.
Butane and Propane Gases.

1954, Precisionwood,
Auburn, MA.
Synthetic Wood Produced
in Sheet Form.

1947, Perfect Circle Corporation,
Hagerstown, IN.
Plastic Gauging Material.

WORLD IMPORTS

1954, Hakato Vinegar Co.,
Handa-Shi, Japan.
Vinegar.

**1956, Schnellpressenfabrik Koenig
& Bauer Aktiengesellschaft,**
Wurzburg, West Germany.
Printing Presses and Graphic
and Stereotyping Machinery.

1954, Frymann and Fletcher Ltd.,
Nottingham, England.
Piece Goods of Silk, Cotton,
Wool, and Worsted Fibers.

1954, Alfred Sternjakob K.G.,
Frankenthal, West Germany.
Extendable Multi-Purpose Bags
and Valises.

1945, Adolph Saurer Co.,
Arbon, Switzerland.
Automobiles, Wheels, Bodies,
and Transmissions.

**1952, E. Mettler, Fabrik für
Analysenwaagen,**
Zurich, Switzerland.
Girdle Webbing.

1957, "Nordsee" Deutsche Hochseefischerer Aktiengesellschaft,
Bremerhaven, West Germany.
Fresh, Fried, Smoked, Frozen, and Preserved Fish.

1954, Stockmann GmbH,
Hamburg-Wandsbek,
West Germany.
Canned Meat, Fish, Fruits,
Vegetables, and Other Food.

1948, Gunther Wagner, S.R.L.,
Buenos Aires, Argentina.
Writing and Drawing Inks.

1950, Syndicat Français,
Paris, France.
Tuxedoes, Underwear,
and Evening Wear.

1950, Syndicat Français,
Paris, France.
Tuxedos, Underwear
and Evening Wear.

1948, Avalon Leather Board Co., Ltd.,
Street, England.
Cellulose Fibers for Use
as a Leather Substitute.

1953, Zellstollfabrik Waldof, Mannheim, West Germany. Pulp Paper and Paper Products.

1954, Gustav August Seewer, Burgdorf, Switzerland. Power Operated Roller-Type Machines for Paper.

1954, Everest Nähmaschinen, Stuttgart, West Germany. Sewing Machines and Parts Thereof.

**1953, Mirna Poduzece
Za Preradbu Ribe,**
Rijeka, Yugoslavia.
Canned Fish.

**1955, Zavody V. I. Lenina Plzen,
Narodm Podnik,**
Plzen, Czechoslovakia.
Electric Motors, Transformers,
and Condensers.

**1953, Mardesic Tvornie
Riblijih Konservi,**
Zadar, Yugoslavia.
Canned Fish.

**1957, Institut Dr. Ing,
Reinhard Straumann,**
Waldenburg, Switzerland.
Parts for Clocks and Watches.

**1957, Agfa Aktiengesellschaft
für Photofabrikation,**
Bayerwerk, West Germany.
Photographic Papers.

1949, The Mountain Copper Co.,
London, England.
Copper Sulfate, Carbonate,
Hydroxide, Iron Oxide, and Pyrites.

1947, Bally's Shoe Factories, Ltd., Zurich, Switzerland. Girdle Webbing.

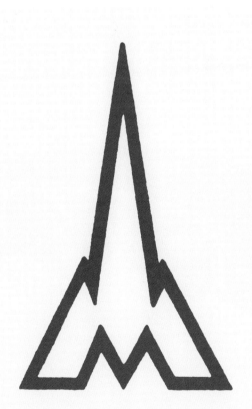

1953, Klockner-Humboldt-Deuts Aktiengesellschaft, Köln-Deutz, Germany. Trucks, Buses, and Ambulances.

1954, S. A. Eteco Co., Zweregem, Belgium. Barbed Wires and Fencing.

1945, Tonsa, Sociedad Anonima Comercial E Industrial, Buenos Aires, Argentina. Shoes, Boots, and Slippers.

1952, Rowntree and Co., London, England. Medicinal Candy Lozenges.

Ben Pieratt
GENERAL PROJECTS

Most of the work in this book is older than I am. Much of it is older than my parents or my parents' parents. You will understand when I say that I hold many of these trademarks in a similar regard as I do my elders. Respect. Admiration. Awe. As I look to both for guidance, they teach the same lessons: Work hard. Have character. Get your hands dirty.

Streamlined times call for streamlined logos, but it is too easy to let the the velocity of our tools seep through into our working methods. Now that we are able to deliver entirely presentable, entirely mediocre logos in less time than ever, we legitimize the claim that our work can be replicated by a niece, nephew, brother, or friend with the right software. What does it tell us that as our tools have gotten easier to use, our logos have gotten easier to replicate?

As apprenticeships continue to go out of style, young designers must take it upon ourselves to find our mentors in the annals of graphic history and look to the efforts of our betters for guidance. Retrospectives such as this are all too valuable in their ability to remind us to pour love and care and craft into our work, ensuring that later generations have equally worthy foundations from which to draw.

2005, Squarewolf.

2006, Friday Mile.

The
Embrella
Group

2006, The Embrella Group.

2008, Monogram.

2006, Lee Reedy Fine Art.

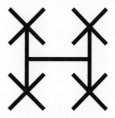

2009, Iridesco, LLC.

2009, Panama.

2004, Readymech.

2009, Oak.fm.

1964, Bathurst Containers, Ltd.,
Montreal, Quebec, Canada.
Shipping Cartons
for Display Purposes.

**1967, Oshino Electric Lamp
Works, Ltd.,**
Tokyo, Japan.
Miniature Electric Lamps.

**1961, Allmånna Svenska
Elektriaska Aktiebolaget,**
Vasteras, Sweden.
Nuclear Reactors.

1967, B. Aprengel & Co.,
Hanover, Germany.
Candy and Confectionery.

**1968, Allied Breweries
(UK) Limited,**
Burton-on-Trent, England.
Ales.

1968, CIBA Ltd.,
Basel, Switzerland.
Chemical Preparations
for Killing Weeds.

1968, Bartson's,
Antwerp, Belgium.
Clothes.

1967, Creations Pierre Ferrat,
Paris, France.
Clothes.

1960, L'Allobroge,
Chambery, France.
Candies.

**1972, Österreichische
Hartkase Export,**
Innsbruck, Austria.
Cheese.

1967, The Dunlop Co., Ltd.,
Birmingham, England.
Life Rafts.

**1960, Etablissements
Chevallier Père,**
Angers, Main-et-Loire, France.
Perfumes.

1963, Oulevay S.A., Morges, Vaud, Switzerland. Biscuits.

1967, Jakob Schlaepfer & Co. AG,
St. Gall, Switzerland.
Embroidery.

**1972, Rud. Starcks
Kommanditgesellschaft,**
Melle, Germany.
Abrasives.

**1973, Expansion
Biologique Francaise,**
Paris, France.
Cosmetics.

**1972, Pulloverånm Sicuedad
Añonima Industrial y Commercial,**
Buenos Aires, Argentina.
Pullovers, Sweaters, Sweatershirts,
Cardigans, and Shawls.

1968, Industri Aktiebolaget,
Nasbypark, Sweden.
Metalworking Machines and Tools.

1977, Rasmus Hansen A/S,
Copenhagen, Denmark.
Cheese.

1962, The Royal Bank of Canada,
Montreal, Quebec, Canada.
Periodical Newsletters.

**1967, The Ceylon Tea
Propaganda Board,**
Colombo, Ceylon.
Tea.

1967, Atlanta Trading Corp.,
New York, NY.
Cheese.

1971, Le Cordon Bleu, S.A.R.L.,
Paris, France.
Educational Services.

**1966, Bårcharciter-Verlag Karl
Vøtterie K.G. Kassel,**
Wilhelmsholie, Germany.
Phonograph Records.

**1978, Glenmac Knitwear
(Hawick), Ltd.,**
Hawick, Scotland.
Knitted Cardigans.

**1973, Atelier Brillen Anton
Auger GmbH,**
Linz, Austria.
Spectacles, Spectacle Frames,
and Sunglasses.

**1970, Artex S.A. Fabrica
de Artefatos Textels,**
Santa Catarina, Brazil.
Beach Wear and Lounge Wear
for Men and Women.

1974, Gaveau-Erard,
Paris, France.
Upright Pianos.

1960, Radiotechnisches Werk,
Esslingen am Neckar, Germany.
Radio Transmission.

**1966, Ceskoslovenske
Cokoladovny,**
Modrany, Czechoslovakia.
Eating, Baking,
and Cooking Chocolate.

**1969, J. Mayer & Sohn-Cornelius
Heyl Lederfabrik AG,**
Worms, Germany.
Kid Leather.

**1974, Franz Carl
Weber-Holding AG,**
Zurich, Switzerland.
Toys.

1976, Pretal S.R.L.,
Buenos Aires, Argentina.
Saddles, Girths, Headstalls,
Stirrup Leathers, Stable Halters,
Martingales, and Reins.

1977, Janssen Pharmaceutica,
Beerse, Belgium.
Pharmaceutical Products
for Human and Veterinary Use.

**1965, Impermeabil San Giorgio
Societa Per Asioni,**
Genoa, Italy.
Clothing.

1976, Manifatture Riabella S.P.A.,
Biella, Italy.
Yarns and Threads.

**1966, Nippon Yusbutan Kinzoku
Yoshiokki Koygyo,**
Niigata-ken, Japan.
Flatware.

1960, Hearmann & Reimer GmbH,
Holzminden, Germany.
Aromatic and Flavoring Substances.

1973, Audi Nau Auto Union Ag.,
Ingolstadt, Germany.
Automobiles.

1977, Rumianca S.P.A.,
Torino, Italy.
Pesticides and Plant
Pharmaceuticals.

1967, Cominco, Ltd.,
Quebec, Canada.
Chemical Fertilizers.

1973, Simpson of Australia, Ltd.,
Victoria, Australia.
Men's and Women's
Sports Clothing.

1976, Unicorn Products, Ltd.,
London, England.
Sporting Goods.

1960, Société Eminence, Nimes, France. Briefs, Waistcoats, and T-Shirts for Men, Women, and Children.

1972, Primrose Sportswear, Ltd., Montreal, Quebec, Canada. Women's Clothes.

EATING AND ENTERTAINMENT

1952, Dormeyer Corp., Chicago, IL. Electrically Operated Deep Fat Fryers.

1945, The W.L. Maxon Corp., New York, NY. Electric Ovens Designed Specifically for Thawing and Cooking Frozen Food.

1952, The Borden Co.,
New York, NY.
Canned, Unbaked Biscuits.

1957, Wilson & Company, Inc.,
Chicago, IL.
Fresh, Cooked, Smoked, Cured
and Frozen Meats.

1952, Douglas Fir Plywood Assoc.,
Tacoma, WA.
Plywood.

1956, Krisp-Pak, Inc.,
New York, NY.
Soup Mix, Cole Slaw,
and Collard Greens.

1954, Gold Prize Coffee Co., Inc.,
Chicago, IL.
Coffee, Tea, Dessert Toppings,
Spices, and Sauces.

1952, Zion Industries, Inc.,
Zion, IL.
Cookies and Cakes with
Candy Fillings and Toppings.

**1954, Certified Grocers
of Illinois, Inc.,**
Chicago, IL.
Information Service to the Trade.

1947, Brice-Waldrop Pickle Co.,
Denison, TX.
Cucumber Pickles.

1947, Wason Brothers Co., Inc.,
Seattle, WA.
Spices, Sauces, and
Food Flavoring Extracts.

1952, Paxton and Gallagher Co.,
Omaha, NE.
Coffee.

1948, Spaulding Bakeries, Inc.,
Binghamton, NY.
Bread and Bakery Products.

1950, Columbia Breweries, Inc.,
Tacoma, WA.
Beer.

1953, Motyer & Clement Ltd.,
East London, Union of South Africa.
Ginger Beer.

**1953, Kwik-Shake Dispenser
Manufacturing Co., Inc.,**
Chicago, IL.
Mixing Unit and Dispenser
for Frozen Ice Cream Mix.

1955, Dog n Suds, Inc.,
Champaign, IL.
Soft Drinks and
Soft Drink Concentrates.

1955, Kellogg Co.,
Battle Creek, MI.
Ready-to-Eat Cereal Food.

1953, Tunies, Inc.,
Chula Vista, CA.
Fish Sausages.

1945, Clougherty Brothers,
Vernon, CA.
Sausage and Other Meat Products.

1951, Piggly Wiggly Corp.,
Jacksonville, FL.
Meats, Fruits, Vegetables, Coffee,
Tea, and Candies.

1950, The Rath Packing Co.,
Waterloo, IA.
Bacon.

1956, The Rath Packing Co.,
Waterloo, IA.
Packaged Meats.

Emily Oberman & Bonnie Siegler
NUMBER 17

As kids, we both loved logos. Inexplicably, we each knew that there was almost nothing more wonderful than a perfect logo. And the logos that we were drawn to helped shape not only who we would become as designers but also what we played with, watched, listened to, read, and wore while we were growing up.

Some of those logos were very famous and others not so much, but each one burned its way into our minds, resulting in certain tendencies we both have today as designers. Weirdly, many (but not all) of them were the same for each of us. So, as a way of giving people a glimpse into what is way down deep inside the minds of a couple of designers, here is a short list of logos and trademarks that continue to influence us every day: Colorforms; Baskin-Robbins (the original design); *The Partridge Family*; Andy Warhol's *Interview* magazine; *Life* magazine; Buster Brown Shoes; *Monty Python's Flying Circus*; *Zoom*; PBS; the Tropicana girl; Atari; Burlington; NASA; Apple Records; *Love, American Style*; and of course the original UPS logo.

And now, as designers, we still find new logos to love and be inspired by, every day. Some are brand new and some are quite old. Some are out there in the world and some are right here in this wonderful book.

2004, Spice Market.

2008, The Daily Beast.

2006, Housing Works.

Lucky.

NATIONAL SEPTEMBER 11
MEMORIAL & MUSEUM
AT THE WORLD TRADE CENTER

1999, Lucky Magazine.

2007, National September 11
Memorial & Museum.

2000, Orbitz.

2007, Saturday Night Live.

2002, Trio.

2005, Air America Radio.

1966, M. Hohner, Inc., Hicksville, NY. Harmonicas.

1965, Hassenfeld Bros., Inc., Pawtucket, RI. Toy Dolls and Accessories.

1965, United Artists Entertainment, New York, NY. Film Production Studio.

1974, Music Man, Inc.,
Anaheim, CA.
Instrumental Speakers
and Amplifiers.

1971, Ovation, Inc.,
Glenview, IL.
Phonograph Records.

1968, Capitol Records, Inc.,
Los Angeles, CA.
Phonograph Records.

1960, The Elektra Corp.,
New York, NY.
Phonograph Records.

1978, Slash Records,
Falls Church, VA.
Phonograph Records.

1966, Screen Gems, Inc.,
New York, NY.
Merchandising Materials
for the Promotion of Films.

1978, Custom Sound, Inc.,
Wichita, KS.
Retail Sound Reproduction.

1964, Children, Inc.,
Beverly Hills, CA.
Phonograph Records.

1973, RSO Records,
London, England.
Phonograph Records
and Tape Recordings.

1977, Average White Band,
Los Angeles, CA.
Performance and
Musical Entertainment.

1978, John Klemmer,
Los Angeles, CA.
Entertainment Services.

1977, Heart,
Seattle, WA.
Entertainment Services.

1966, Screen Gems, Inc.,
New York, NY.
Musical Entertainment Services.

1974, Motown Records Corp.,
Detroit, MI.
Entertainment Services.

1974, Rock Steady, Inc.,
New York, NY.
Musical Entertainment Services.

1975, Grateful Dead Productions,
San Rafael, CA.
T-Shirt and Entertainment Services.

1978, Paramount Picture Corp.,
New York, NY.
Merchandising Materials
for the Promotion of Films.

1977, Starland Vocal Band,
Bethesda, MD.
Entertainment Services.

1969, Laugh-In Restaurant Corp.,
Miami, FL.
Restaurant Services.

1964, Hawk Model Co., Inc.,
Chicago, IL.
Toys.

1971, Carefree Travel, Inc.,
New York, NY.
Travel Services to Las Vegas.

1967, Topps Chewing Gum, Inc.,
Brooklyn, NY.
Chewing Gum.

**1970, Doris Moore
of California, Inc.,**
Long Beach, CA.
Bathing Suits, Jackets, and Shirts.

1977, Tyco Industries, Inc.,
Moorestown, NJ.
Train Set.

1964, Louis Marx & Co., Inc.,
New York, NY.
Toy Sport Car Racing Sets.

1976, En-Jay International, Ltd.,
College Park, MD.
Beverage Recipe Cards.

1974, R.F.R., Inc.,
Hope, RI.
Recreational Vehicles.

1961, Fair Lanes, Inc., Baltimore, MD. Bowling Alley Services.

**1975, Control Products
Surfing Equipment,**
Venice, CA.
Sports Equipment and Accessories.

**1979, First American
Warranty Corp.,**
Kansas City, MO.
Underwriting Maintenance
and Repair Insurance for
Motorcycle Owners.

1969, Hockey Club of Pittsburgh,
Pittsburgh, PA.
Professional Ice Hockey Games.

1960, John Souza,
Oakland, CA.
Salad Dressing and Sauces.

1961, Foodmaker Co.,
San Diego, CA.
Restaurant Services.

1972, Burger King Corp.,
Miami, FL.
Restaurant Services.

1972, Reynolds Metals Co.,
Richmond, VA.
Aluminum Foil.

1971, Automatic Service Co.,
Atlanta, GA.
Brownies.

1968, Mr. Donut of America, Inc.,
Westwood, MA.
Fillings for Donuts.

1974, Dunkin' Donuts of America,
Randolph, MA.
Donuts.

**1960, Tennessee Products
and Chemical Corp.,**
Nashville, TN.
Charcoal Briquettes.

1978, The Domal Group,
Los Angeles, CA.
Donuts.

1921, The American Paint Works, New Orleans, LA. Dry Paste and Ready-Mixed Paints.

1928, Walter E. Disney, Hollywood, CA. Motion Pictures Reproduced in Copies for Sale.

1937, Paul Gibson,
Richmond, VA.
Automotive Windshield
Cleaning Products.

1929, Waco Coffee Co., Inc.,
Waco, TX.
Coffee.

1930, Steel Publications, Inc.,
Pittsburgh, PA.
Periodical.

1939, Fisher Bros. Paper Co., Inc.,
Fort Wayne, IN.
Matches.

1938, Louis L. Jacob, Inc.,
Orlando, FL.
Fresh Citrus Fruits.

1937, Popular Brands, Inc.,
Wyncote, PA.
Detergent Preparation
for Dish Washing.

1939, Grandpa Brands Co.,
Cincinnati, OH.
Nonalcoholic Maltless Beverages
Sold as Soft Drinks.

1927, Tacoma Brewing Co.,
San Francisco, CA.
Cereal Malt Beverages.

1929, Atlas Engineering Co.,
Clintonville, WI.
Concrete Mixers and Belt,
Bucket, and Brick Conveyors.

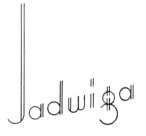

1935, Viennese Laboratories, Inc.,
Brooklyn, NY.
Talcum, Body Powder, Toothpaste,
Shampoo, and Hair Tonic.

1938, Schaeffer Products Co.,
Cleveland, OH.
Prophylactic Rubber Articles
for the Prevention
of Contagious Diseases.

1938, Pohatcong Hosiery Mills, Inc.,
Washington, NJ.
Ladies' Full Fashioned Silk Hosiery.

1938, Tremont Mills Corp.,
New York, NY.
French Trimming Ribbon for Hats,
Dresses, and Blouses.

1929, The Yantic Grain & Products Co.,
Norwich, CT.
Intermediate Chick Feed, Growing
Feed, and Hog Feed.

1936, Ludwig Lustig,
New York, NY.
Internal-Combustion Engines
and Parts Thereof.

1937, The Collins Co.,
Clinton, IA.
Fly Swatters.

1935, The Coffield Protector Co.,
Dayton, OH.
Lubricating Oil Compounds.

1934, Zingo Co.,
New York, NY.
Toy Pistol.

1921, Fisheries Products Co., Inc., New York. NY. Fertilizers.

1926, H. P. Ulich & Co., New York, NY. Necktie Boxes and Display Cards.

1938, Philomené G. Walsh, Chicago, IL. Sauce for Vegetables, Puddings, Soups, and Meats.

1925, Jiffy Manufacturing Co.,
Huron, SD.
Liquid for Stopping Leaks
in Radiators.

1937, Household Utilities Corp.,
Chicago, IL.
Clothes Dryer.

1932, Utility Manufacturing Co., Inc.,
New York, NY.
Photographic Cameras
and Parts Thereof.

1938, Jingle Bell Ice Cream Co.,
Fort Worth, TX.
Ice Cream Bars.

1935, Busy Bee Specialties Co.,
Chicago, IL.
Candied Popcorn Confections.

1938, Morrison Engineering Co., Inc.,
Cleveland, OH.
Ovens.

1936, Daubert and Knight, Columbus, OH. Medicinal Preparations.

JP Williams
DESIGN MW

I first became aware of marks because of a family crest. An uncle had done a comprehensive investigation of our family tree and the result was a book that traced us back to somewhere in Wales. That book sat in our den and I would look through it periodically and stare at the family crest on the title page. Since that time I have been interested in marks, whether they were maker's marks, printer marks, merchant marks, even initials.

Some beloved marks include Paul Rand's ABC, William Golden's CBS, Will Burtin's International Paper, Sutnar's Sweets. We all have our favorites. Mine has always been Piet Zwart's own identity. A simple *P* and a black square. These designs have the characteristics essential to the success of any mark; they are all memorable, timeless, evocative, simple, different, smart, and unusual.

The marks I selected for this book share these qualities. Each mark begins with the client's wish to communicate its point of view and reassure the audience that they have something in common, a shared interest or sensibility. In the case of B Braithwaite, a children's store, a subtle nod to a teddy bear adds humor and a smile. Whereas the logo for ab initio, a software company, uses basic elements that underscore their core message.

It is wonderful to be a contributor to the rich history of trademark design. The early volumes are a wonderful reference, worthy of visiting time and again.

2003, Maclaren.

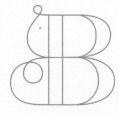

2005, B Braithwaite.

LUQUE

2002, Luque.

brocade HOME

2006, Brocade Home.

THE
SHADE
STORE

2007, The Shade Store.

GMUND
BLANC
beige

2002, Gmund Blanc Beige.

Ab InITIO

2001, Ab Initio.

2005, Organic Bouquet.

west elm

2003, West Elm.

1931, Southern Oak Flooring Industries, Little Rock, AR. Flooring—Namely, Tongued and Grooved, End-Matched, Square Edge Strips, Parquetry, and Fabricated Blocks.

1937, Zeen Chemical Co.,
Cleveland, OH.
Dry Cleaning Fluids,
Rug and Carpet Shampoos.

1920, Consumers Brewing Co.,
Philadelphia, PA.
Cereal Beverages Made of Malt.

1925, The George W. Luft Co., Inc.,
New York, NY.
Day, Night, and Cleansing Creams.

1929, William G. Roe,
Winter Haven, FL.
Fresh Citrus Fruits.

1929, Whitemore Brothers Corp.,
Cambridge, MA.
Ice Cream and Dressing.

1927, Elting Brothers,
New York, NY.
Men's and Women's Hosiery.

1934, American Record Corp.,
New York, NY.
Phonograph Needles.

1925, Edgar-Morgan Co.,
Memphis, TN.
Feeds and Foodstuffs for Poultry,
Cattle, Horses, Mules, and Hogs.

**1929, Permatite Manufacturing
Co. Inc.,**
Minneapolis, MN.
Electrical Crankcase Heaters.

1954, Union Bag & Paper Corp.,
New York, NY.
Semi-Chemical
Corrugating Medium.

1952, Koch Engineering Co., Inc.,
Wichita, KS.
Petroleum Refinery Apparatus
and Parts Thereof.

1948, Kryptar Corp.,
Rochester, NY.
Photographic Film.

1948, Kemart Corp.,
San Francisco, CA.
Drawing Papers
and Illustration Boards.

1950, Knoll Associates, Inc.,
New York, NY.
Tables, Desks, Seats, Stools,
Sofas, Beds, Chests,
Cabinets, and Trays.

1950, Basil L. Smith System,
Philadelphia, PA.
Engraving Pictures,
Designs, and Images.

1952, McGraw Electric Co.,
Milwaukee, WI.
Electrical Conductor Connectors.

1956, Kiekhaefer Corp.,
Cedarburg, WI.
Oil.

1952, Kerr Wire Products Co.,
Chicago, IL.
Display Stands, Racks, and Shelves.

1954, Knoll Associates, Inc., New York, NY. Curtain and Upholstery Fabrics.

polk·a dot

1948, Certified Dry Mat Corp., New York, NY. Matrix Dry Mat, or Board Used in Stereotyping.

1955, Sunbeam Corp.,
Chicago, IL.
Electric Water Kettles
and Tea Brewing Apparatus.

1955, Wire Specialties Co.,
Santa Clara, CA.
Cooking Grills.

1954, American Alcolac Corp.,
Baltimore, MD.
Detergents for Industrial Use.

1957, Colgate-Palmolive Co.,
New York, NY.
Sudsing Cleansers and Detergents.

1952, Wholesale Sales Co.,
Wilmington, DE.
Automotive Polish.

1955, Norcross, Inc.,
New York, NY.
Greeting Cards and Printed
Greeting Folders.

1955, Carl M. Friedel,
Pocatello, ID.
Game and Game Pieces.

1956, Hancock Corp.,
Philadelphia, PA.
Scrub Mops with
Absorbent Material.

1956, Stanson Chemicals,
Edgewater, NJ.
Detergent for Washing Clothes,
Dishes, and Painted Surfaces.

Michael Doret
MICHAEL DORET GRAPHIC DESIGN

Most of the wonderful trademarks compiled in this collection share one unfortunate trait: the names of the men and women who brought them to life are mostly forgotten. But through these marks, as represented by this collection, they have left a rich graphic legacy that was a strong force in shaping my aesthetics and my graphic vision, as well as those of many of my contemporaries.

Some of these trademarks are real prize-winners; many are quirky, some even downright awkward, but almost all of them joyously display a flagrant lack of regard for what some would consider to be "the formal rules of design." It is precisely this freewheeling, almost "anything goes" attitude that gives these marks their energy. I imagine that these artists were just doing what came naturally; they may not have known the rules, so how could they have known they were breaking them? It is these "mistakes," these flourishes typographic and pictorial, that I find so engaging, and that I've tried to pay homage to in my own design work. This collection represents a rich graphic vocabulary that still resonates in today's digital culture. Some call it "vintage." I call it vital and alive, bearing the imprint of the maker's hand. I would be satisfied if I could get but a small portion of the fun, the irreverence, the blissful lack of self-consciousness of this work into my own.

So I salute all of them, those designers, those nameless unsung heroes of mine, for without their accomplishments and without being able to go through the doors they unknowingly pried open, what I do might never have been possible.

2006, Tribeca Film Festival.

1997, Coolsville Records.

2000, uMogul.com.

1980, Graphic Artists Guild.

2000, Hollywood and Vine.

1997, Local Flavors QVC.

1996, Storyville Post
MVP Creative LLC.

1999, Knicks National
Basketball Association.

2006, Alphabet Soup,
Type Founders.

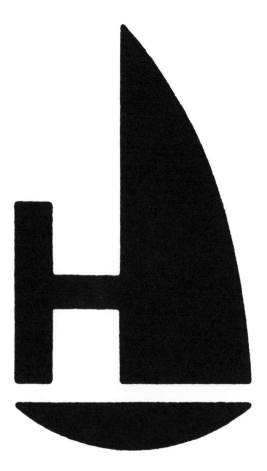

1957, Holiday Yachts, Inc., Centerport, NY. Sailboats and Power Boats.

1948, Holgate Brothers Co., Kane, PA. Educational Toys.

Fur.Sheen

1954, Walter Haertel Co., Minneapolis, MN. Fur Cleaning and Glazing Compound.

1947, Gibson, Inc., Kalamazoo, MI. Guitars, Mandolins, Violins, and Banjos.

1953, Hassenfield Brothers, Inc.,
Central Falls, RI.
Toy Kit Containing Figure
with Plastic Removable Body Parts.

1952, Bluhil Foods, Inc.,
Denver, CO.
Salted Nuts.

1955, Vital Publications, Inc.,
New York, NY.
Cartoon Booklets.

1952, Beaunit Mills, Inc.,
New York, NY.
Thread and Yarn.

1958, L-J Enterprises, Inc.,
Boulder, CO.
General Chemical
Cleaning Preparations.

1945, Gray-Mills Co.,
Evanston, IL.
Refrigerating Apparatus.

1957, Fairway Foods, Inc.,
St. Paul, MN.
Coffee.

1957, W. L. Ollinghouse,
Little Rock, AR.
Fishing Boats.

1953, Dallas Iron & Wire Works, Inc.,
Dallas, TX.
Swings, Gliders, Gyms,
and Exercise Frames.

1948, Strobo Research,
Milwaukee, WI.
Photographic Equipment.

1949, Crown Zellerbach Corp.,
San Francisco, CA.
Toilet Tissue.

1953, Mid-States Corp.,
Chicago, IL.
House Trailers.

1956, Astatic Corp.,
Conneaut, OH.
Microphones for Radio
and Television Broadcasting.

1951, Specialty Battery Co.,
Madison, WI.
Dry Cells, Dry Cell Batteries,
and Battery Packs.

1958, Data Products, Inc.,
Hartford, CT.
Printed Checks, Check Books,
and Bank Stationery.

1946, Westelectric Castings, Inc.,
Los Angeles, CA.
Steel Castings.

1946, Electronic Rectifiers, Inc.,
Indianapolis, IN.
Electronic Rectifiers.

1949, Hubbard and Co.,
Pittsburgh, PA.
Anchor Rods, Eye Bolts, Clamps,
Brackets, and Braces.

1953, Dorse and Margolin, Inc., Westbury, NY. High-Frequency Antennas.

1947, Picture Recording Co., Oconomowoc, WI. Picture Reproduction for Use with a Stereopticon Projector.

1957, Technical Marketing Associates, Inc., Concord, MA. Integrated Marketing Services.

1955, Keeshan-Miller Enterprises,
New York, NY.
Title for Television Show
Featuring Puppets, Story Telling,
and Farm Animals.

1956, Nutrition Square, Inc.,
Pittsburgh, PA.
Vitamin and Mineral
Food Supplements.

1955, Washington Aluminum Co., Inc.,
Baltimore, MD.
Gangways, Shiftable Steps,
and Hatch Covers.

1950, Baracuta Ltd.,
Manchester, UK
Trousers, Overcoats, Capes,
and Other Apparel Items.

1957, Hi-Line Company, Inc.,
New York, NY.
Infants' and Children's Apparel.

1955, Homalite Corp.,
Wilmington, DE.
Clear Cast Plastic Sheet Material.

1945, Queen City Cuttery Co.,
Titusville, PA.
Pen Knives, Shears,
and Kitchen Knives.

1950, Arrow Manufacturing Co.,
West New York, NJ.
Plastic Cases Designed
for Holding Watches.

1946, The Green Co., Inc.,
Kansas City, MO.
Jewelry and Personal Wear.

1949, Summer Chemical Co.,
Zeeland, MI.
Chemical Compounds.

1955, Eska Co.,
Dubuque, IA.
Scale Model Miniature Tractors,
Hay Loaders, Crawlers, Wagons,
and Plows.

1956, H. F. Stimm, Inc.,
Buffalo, NY.
Construction and Repair
of Buildings, Bridges, and Roads.

1955, Grace Chemical Co.,
New York, NY.
Urea Feed Compounds.

1953, Ansul Chemical Co.,
Marinette, WI.
Portable Hand- and Wheel-Mounted
Fire-Extinguishers.

1946, Westelectric Castings, Inc.,
Los Angeles, CA.
Steel Castings.

1954, Colgate-Palmolive Co.,
Jersey City, NJ.
Sudsing Cleaner, Cleanser,
and Detergent.

1955, Inland Electronics Corp.,
Aurora, IL.
Design and Development
of Electronic Products.

1955, Tom Daly Electric, Inc.,
Barberton, OH.
Detergent for Automatic
Washing Machines.

1957, The Lummus Co.,
Chemical and Petroleum Distillation,
Refinery Apparatus and Equipment.

1956, Foremost Dairies, Inc.,
San Francisco, CA.
Butter, Milk, Ice Cream, and Eggs.

1956, Phillips Packing Co., Inc.,
Cambridge, MA.
Canned Soups, Vegetables,
and Beans.

1956, Automotive Products, Inc.,
Portland, OR.
Apparatus for Testing
and Analyzing Diesel Fuel Pumps.

1951, Peterson Welding Labs, Inc.,
Kansas City, MO.
Valve Seat Inserts.

1948, Toy Corporation of America,
Leominster, MA.
Plastic Ducks and Other
Water Fowl in Caricature Form.

1975, The Love Co., Sioux Falls, SD. All-Purpose Cleaning Preparations.

1969, Educational Research Associates, Inc., Palo Alto, CA. Consultation in Internal Administrative Systems.

1967, Avant-Garde Media, Inc.,
New York, NY.
Magazine.

1976, Nichibei Fuji Cycle Co. Ltd.,
Tokyo, Japan.
Bicycle and Structural Parts.

1970, Hanes Corp.,
Winston-Salem, NC.
Women's Hosiery and Pantyhose.

**1976, National Aeronautics
and Space Administration,**
Washington, D.C.
U.S. Government Space
Exploration Program.

1976, American Can Co.,
Greenwich, CT.
Disposable Eating Utensils.

1977, The Gap Stores, Inc.,
San Francisco, CA.
Retail Clothing Store Service.

1978, Walgreen Laboratories, Inc.,
Dearfield, IL.
Deodorant.

1962, The Peppermint Co.,
Philadelphia, PA.
Hoop Made for Dancing the Twist.

1965, Five Notes, Inc.,
Milwaukee, WI.
Entertainment Services.

1976, Pepsico, Inc.,
Purchase, NY.
Soft Drinks and Syrups.

1966, Midland Shoe Co.,
St. Louis, MO.
Women's Shoes.

1971, BIT, Inc.,
Natick, MA.
Installation and Repair Services
for Computers.

1972, Five-y Manufacturing Co.,
Inman, KS.
Riding Power Lawn Mowers.

1976, Claeys Candy, Inc.,
South Bend, IN.
Boxed Chocolate Candy.

1976, National Presto Industries, Inc.,
Eau Claire, WI.
Domestic Electric Cooking Devices.

1977, Fabergé, Inc.,
New York, NY.
T-Shirts.

1977, Hub Distributing, Inc.,
Ontario, CA.
Clothing.

1975, International Typeface Corp.,
New York, NY.
Periodical Journal.

1973, Playgirl Figure Salons,
South Bend, IN.
Conducting Women's
Exercise Workshops.

1972, Williamhouse-Regency, Inc.,
New York, NY.
Greeting Cards.

1961, Susan Thomas,
New York, NY.
Rayon Fabrics Made
into Finished Clothing.

1977, Mather Federal Credit Union,
Sacramento, CA.
Banking Services.

1965, Aims Foundations, Inc.,
New York, NY.
Women's Undergarments.

1969, Nu-Living, Inc.,
North Royalton, OH.
Cosmetic Face
and Body Freshening.

1977, Fabergé, Inc., New York, NY. Cosmetics and Toilet Preparations.

1961, Crown Zellerbach Corp., San Francisco, CA. Polyethylene-Coated Paper Bags.

1972, Second Look, Inc., King of Prussia, PA. Retail Women's Clothing Store Services.

1966 Arthur Taylor Lee, Los Angeles, CA. Musical Entertainment Services.

1969, M.T.S. Productions, Cincinnati, OH. Automobile Bumper Stickers.

1968, Brattle Films, Inc., Cambridge, MA. Men's and Women's Clothing Apparel.

1964, Hawk Model Co., Inc.,
New York, NY.
Plastic Juvenile Luggage
and School Bags.

1962, The Hubbard-Hall Chemical Co.,
Waterbury, CT.
Fertilizers.

1960, Charles A. Crete,
Marysville, CA.
Multi-Vitamin Preparation
for Children.

1974, The Whiz Kids,
Chicago, IL.
Artistic Design of Commercial
Printing Media.

1969, Southwestern Apparel, Inc.,
Garland, TX.
Women's Slacks, Blouses, Skirts,
Dresses, and Jackets.

1976, Citicorp,
New York, NY.
Leasing Space
for Commercial Outlets.

1972, Williamhouse-Regency, Inc.,
New York, NY.
Greeting Cards.

1969, Precision Merchandise, Inc.,
Brooklyn, NY.
Cologne.

1969, Freeman Enterprises, Inc.,
New York, NY.
Men's Clothing.

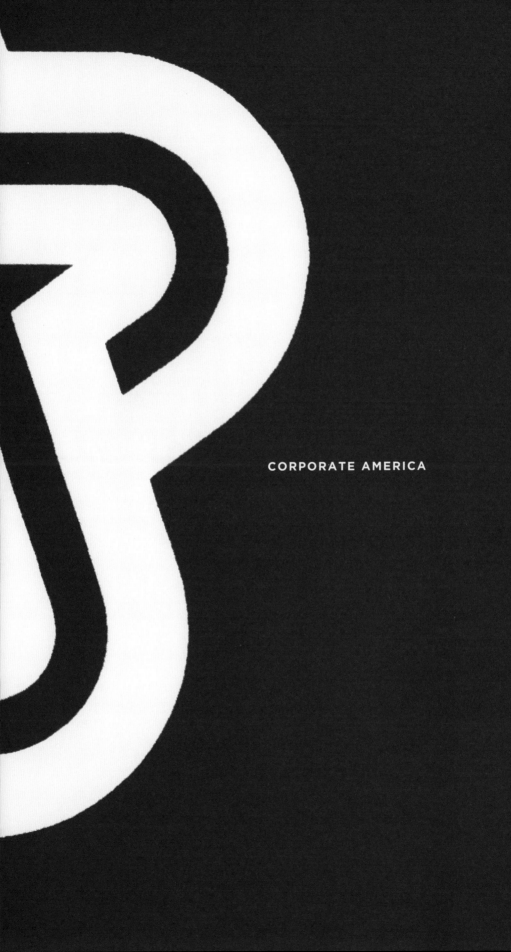

CORPORATE AMERICA

1945, Metropolitan Watch Material Importing Co., New York, NY. Watch Finding, Movements, and Parts Thereof.

**1940, Columbia Broadcasting
System, Inc.,**
New York, NY.
Phonograph Records.

**1947, National Broadcasting
Co., Inc.,**
New York, NY.
Radio Sound Broadcasting
and Recorded Radio Programs.

1952, Volvo,
Chicago, IL.
Gas, Oil, and Other
Automotive Products.

1957, Pillsbury Mills, Inc.,
Minneapolis, MN.
Flour, Refrigerated Doughs
for Cookies, Cakes, Waffles,
and Pancakes.

1949, Capitol Records, Inc.,
Los Angeles, CA.
Grooved Phonograph Records.

1952, Serta Associates, Inc.,
Wilmington, DE.
Mattresses.

1956, Bausch & Lomb Optical Co.,
Rochester, NY
Sunglasses, Shooting Glasses,
and Ophthalmic Lenses.

1958, Lockheed Aircraft and Corp.,
Burbank, CA.
Airplanes and Components Thereof.

1949, Hall Brothers, Inc.,
Kansas City, MO.
Greeting Cards.

Stephen Doyle
DOYLE PARTNERS

You just get one chance to make a first impression, and that's where logos come in. Humans have stature, hairstyles, eyewear, clothes, facial expressions, accents, body language, and, importantly, footwear that all help to identify and differentiate us. Companies have trucks. Or business cards. Or packages. Or signs. Or brochures. But rarely do they have all of these together at the same time. Trademarks serve the critical purpose of identifying and connecting. A name can identify, but a trademark does it in a visual way that carries the narrative about the company like a mantle.

A good logo is something that is memorable enough that people should be kind of able to draw it. Not that they should be able to accurately render it, but the premise should be clear enough to be able to be described. Likewise, the colors in it should be distinct enough to be able to be named. Accurate or not, it doesn't matter, but people do not like colors that they cannot identify. It's kind of like Adam and Eve naming the animals after creation. Once they could name everything they saw, that gave them dominion over creation. (And look how that turned out!) But the idea of dominion rules, whether discussing wildebeests or corporate branding. Everyone likes to know what they're looking at.

I like logos that are friendly. The ones that say, "Hello!" I like logos with depth, transparency, color or a nice drawing, or a combination of these elements. And I guess that's because I'm a sucker for stories—the kind you get from studying a stranger at a distance.

2009, Sea Glass.

2005, Top of the Rock.

1989, The World
Financial Center.

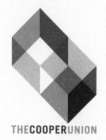

2009, The Cooper Union.

2005, Tishman Speyer.

2007, Martha Stewart.

2005, U.S. Green
Building Council.

1998, Barnes & Noble.

2001, St. Regis
Hotels & Resorts.

1971, Larson Entertainment, Inc.,
Los Angeles, CA.
Photographic Light-Reflecting Devices.

**1970, United States
Automobile Association,**
San Antonio, TX.
Insurance Underwriting
and Estate Planning.

1979, Transamerica Corp.,
San Francisco, CA.
Insurance and Investment Services.

**1970, North American
Rockwell Corp.,**
Pittsburgh, PA.
Structural Parts and Components
for Aerospace and Weapon Defense.

1964, The Wool Bureau, Inc.,
New York, NY.
Products Made Wholly
or Predominantly of Wool.

1972, Continental Airlines, Inc.,
Los Angeles, CA.
Air Transportation.

1970, The Rustix,
Rochester, NY.
Entertainment Services.

**1969, The Torrington
Manufacturing Co.,**
Torrington, CT.
Devices For Propelling Air
and Other Gases.

**1967, Metropolitan
Life Insurance Co.,**
New York, NY.
Insurance and
Annuity Underwriting.

1966, Sea and Ski Corp.,
Millbrae, CA.
Sunglasses.

1977, Control Data Corp.,
Minneapolis, MN.
Paper Goods and Printed Matter.

1969, Crown Zellerbach Corp.,
San Francisco, CA.
Paper Products.

**1977, First Tennessee
National Corp.,**
Memphis, TN.
Banking Services.

**1974, Michael Business
Machines Corp.,**
New York, NY.
Desktop Collators for Sorting
and Distributing Papers.

1969, Analog Technology Corp.,
Pasadena, CA.
Pulse Height Analyzers
and Gas Chromatographs.

**1975, Bay Area Association
For Suicide Prevention,**
San Francisco, CA.
Suicide Prevention.

1960, Allstate Insurance Co.,
Skokie, IL.
Underwriting of Insurance Risks.

**1975, National Congress
of Parents and Teachers,**
Chicago, IL.
Association Services.

1979, American Telephone and Telegraph Co., New York, NY. Telephone Directories.

**1961, The Columbia Broadcasting
System, Inc.,**
New York, NY.
Phonograph Records.

1971, Parasol Press, Ltd.,
New York, NY.
Books and Portfolios
of Original Lithographs.

1960, Lawry's Foods, Inc.,
Los Angeles, CA.
Powdered Dip Mixes, Seasonings,
and Salad Dressings.

1965, Merck & Co., Inc.,
Rahway, NJ.
Pharmaceutical Preparations.

1968, The Quaker Oats Co.,
Chicago, IL.
Ready-to-Eat Cereals.

1971, Eastman Kodak Co.,
Rochester, NY.
Film and Film-Related Products.

1968, Diamond National Corp.,
New York, NY.
Wooden Spoons, Forks,
and Stirrers.

1967, Wescor Corp.,
Hawesville, KY.
Semichemical Corrugating
Medium Material.

**1962, Association of Better
Business Bureaus, Inc.**
New York, NY.
Investigative and Information
Services Relative to Business.

1967, Color Monitor Corp.,
Rye, NY.
Reproducing Documents
and Papers.

1965, Liberty Carton Co.,
Minneapolis, MN.
Insulated Shipping Cartons.

1968, National Nuclear Corp.,
Palo Alto, CA.
Nuclear Reactor
Consulting Services.

**1975, Society of Teachers
of Family Medicine,**
Kansas City, MO.
Association Services.

1966, The Isaly Dairy Corp.,
Youngstown, OH.
Retail Food Store Services.

**1960, American Home
and Lighting Institute,**
Chicago, IL.
Residential Lighting Fixtures.

1960, Motorola, Inc.,
Chicago, IL.
Radio and Television Receiving
and Transmitting Apparatus.

**1974, Huntington Mechanical
Laboratories, Inc.,**
Mountain View, CA.
Construction Services.

1963, Delcon Corp.,
Palo Alto, CA.
Electrical Measuring Devices.

Paula Scher
PENTAGRAM

In the '80s, I used to flip through Eric Baker and Tyler Blik's trademark books for pleasure and for inspiration. So many of the logos were simple and stylistically beautiful. Others were complex, illustrative, and very specific in relationship to their client and audience. And still others were humorous, absurd, or downright goofy.

I really didn't design many identities in the '80s. Trademarks were retro and had a great impact on a lot of my work on book jackets or promotion pieces in the '80s.

Now almost everything I design is some form of identity system. I confess that I seldom concentrate on the design of a trademark purely by itself. A logo or mark is always linked to a broader kit of parts that can be played out over diversified media. Because the systems tend to be complex, the logos I design are often ridiculously simple. I can't imagine that the work in this book is relatable to the way that I currently approach identities. But on second thought, that's why I am going to pay attention to these trademarks all over again.

2008, Truvia.

1998, Citi.

2001, The New 42nd Street.

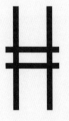

2001, Friends of the High Line.

1984, Manhattan Records.

2006, The Metropolitan Opera.

2008, New York City Ballet.

2006, The Criterion Collection.

2008, The Public.

1969, Stop and Shop, Inc.,
Boston, MA.
Supermarket Services.

1967, Westinghouse Electric Corp.,
Pittsburgh, PA.
Electrical Apparatus, Machines,
and Supplies.

1962, General Foods Corp.,
White Plains, NY.
Processed Foods.

1964, Marine Midland Corp.,
Buffalo, NY.
General Banking Services.

1975, Dann II Morris,
Portland, OR.
Backpacks.

1977, Label Art, Inc.,
Wilton, NH.
Labels.

1970, Castle, Ltd.
Los Angeles, CA.
Envelopes, Writing Paper,
and Correspondence Cards.

**1968, Open Road
International, Inc.,**
St. Louis, MO.
Arranging Travel Tours.

1971, The National Foundation,
White Plains, NY.
Publications—Namely, Pamphlets
and Brochures Related to the
Prevention of Birth Defects.

1962, Safeco Insurance Company of America, Seattle, WA. Underwriting of Insurance.

1961, Scroll Film Industries, Inc.,
New York, NY.
Projectors.

1968, R.D. Products, Inc.,
East Rochester, NY.
Identification Cards.

1972, Watchguard Corp.,
Westport, CT.
Installation of Property
Protection Devices.

1975, Communications Week,
New York, NY.
Communication Conference.

1976, Chemed Corp.,
Cincinnati, OH.
Chemicals.

EXPO'70

1970, Japan World Exposition,
Osaka, Japan.
1970 World Exposition.

1976, Chestel, Inc.,
Chester, CT.
Telephone Communication Systems.

1965, Ames American,
North Easton, MA.
Cleaning and Surfacing
of Rolls Used on Paper Making
and Textile Machinery.

1977, Vita Plus, Inc.,
Las Vegas, NV.
Dietary Supplements.

1969, Allied Van Lines, Inc.,
Broadview, IL.
Packing, Storage,
and Transportation of Goods.

1977, Bergstrom Paper Co.,
Neenah, WI.
Paper Made From Recycled Papers.

1961, Weyerhaeuser Co.,
Tacoma, WA.
Boxes.

1976, Sunkist Growers, Inc., Sherman Oaks, CA. Fruit and Fruit Juices.

1976, Goolagong, Cleveland, OH. Clothes.

**1969, Joint Cling Peach
Advisory Board,**
San Francisco, CA.
Canned California Cling Peaches.

1964, The American Tobacco Co.,
New York, NY.
Cigarettes.

1978, Gro Group, Inc,
Waltham, MA.
Advertising
and Promotional Services.

1972, Nutrition Laboratories, Inc.,
Portland, OR.
Feed Supplement Including
Bacteria Culture.

1974, Philadelphia '76, Inc.,
Philadelphia, PA.
Developing and Directing Plans,
Programs, and Activities
for the Commemoration
of the Bicentennial.

1965, Hunt Foods, Inc.,
Fullerton, CA.
Tomato Products.

1970, Bank of America,
San Francisco, CA.
Commercial Bank Services.

1967, Security First National Bank,
Los Angeles, CA.
Bank Services.

1967, Burlington Industries,
New York, NY.
Finished Fabrics
Used in Men's, Women's,
and Children's Apparel.

1976, Public Broadcasting System, Washington, D.C.
Broadcasting of Educational and Cultural Television Programming.

1976, American Revolution Bicentennial Administration, Washington, D.C.
Commemoration of American Bicentennial.